holiday COOKING

VOLUME 2

DIABETIC LIVING™ HOLIDAY COOKING IS
PART OF A BOOK SERIES PUBLISHED BY
BETTER HOMES AND GARDENS SPECIAL
INTEREST MEDIA, DES MOINES, IOWA

Chocolate-Orange Custards
recipe, page 106

(a time for joy)

There's much to delight in during holiday seasons—especially celebrating with the important people in your life. Loved ones and festivities go together—just like turkey and stuffing, mashed potatoes and gravy, and cookies and sprinkles.

When you or someone in your family is a person living with diabetes (PWD), you can continue to make food an important part of your holiday traditions. For me, certain recipes bring warm memories of shared celebrations. Crunchy, sweet Waldorf salad and creamy banana pudding always call to mind my great-grandmother, Gaigy. Grandma Barbara made rich pumpkin and pecan pies (during one memorable Thanksgiving, our dog, Ruby, climbed up on the table and ate just the centers while the rest of the family was conversing in the living room!). Grandpa, who was a cook in the Army Air Corps during World War II, rolled up his sleeves and washed the dishes after each big holiday meal. I've always been grateful that they kept my diabetes in mind by adapting recipes that I could enjoy along with the rest of the family.

The recipes in this book—all approved by the Better Homes and Gardens Test Kitchen®—have been designed to be lighter in calories, carbohydrates, and sodium but with the full flavor of the foods you love. Now you can enjoy your favorites and stick to your meal plan.

The convenient menus in our "Celebration Menus" chapter allow you to spend less time planning and more time enjoying your gatherings. Recipes from the "Slow-Cooker Meals" chapter free you to take part in even more of the fun. I wish you many more warm, loving holiday memories inspired by the recipes in this cookbook.

Kelly Rawlings

Kelly Rawlings
PWD type 1, Editor
Diabetic Living® magazine

ON THE COVER:
Traditional Roast Turkey (recipe, page 8)

Photographer: Scott Little
Food stylist: Dianna Nolin

Editorial Director JOHN RIHA
Creative Director BRIDGET SANDQUIST

Editor KELLY RAWLINGS
Design Director TED ROSSITER

Contributing Editor KRISTI THOMAS, R.D.
Senior Associate Editor RACHEL MARTIN
Contributing Copy Editor GRETCHEN KAUFFMAN
Contributing Proofreader JEAN BAKER
Test Kitchen Director LYNN BLANCHARD
Test Kitchen Product Supervisor LAURA MARZEN, R.D.
Administrative Assistant MARLENE TODD
Editorial Assistant SHERI CORD
Business Office Assistant SHARON LEIN

Senior Associate Art Director MICHELLE BILYEU
Contributing Designer JILL BUDDEN
Graphic Designer RACHEL DIERENFIELD

EDITORIAL ADMINISTRATION

Managing Editor KATHLEEN ARMENTROUT
Copy Chief DOUG KOUMA
Office Manager CINDY SLOBASZEWSKI
Senior Copy Editors KEVIN COX
JENNIFER SPEER RAMUNDT
ELIZABETH KEEST SEDREL
Assistant Copy Editor METTA CEDERDAHL

EDITORIAL SERVICES

Senior Director of Premedia/Quality Operations STEVE JOHNSON
Director of Premedia Services PENNY SULLIVAN
Photo Studio Manager JEFF ANDERSON **Color Quality Analyst** TONY HUNT
Prepress Desktop Specialist RYAN ALEXANDER

CONSUMER MARKETING

Vice President, Consumer Marketing DAVE BALL
Consumer Products Marketing Director STEVE SWANSON
Consumer Product Associate Marketing Manager WENDY MERICAL
Business Manager DARREN TOLLEFSON

MEREDITH PUBLISHING GROUP

President JACK GRIFFIN
Chief Revenue Officer TOM HARTY **Finance and Administration** MIKE RIGGS
Manufacturing BRUCE HESTON **Consumer Marketing** DAVE BALL
Corporate Sales MICHAEL BROWNSTEIN **Meredith 360°** JACK BAMBERGER
Interactive Media DOUG OLSON **Interactive Media Sales** LAUREN WIENER
Corporate Marketing NANCY WEBER **Research** BRITTA WARE
Chief Technology Officer TINA STEIL **New Media Marketing Services** ANDY WILSON

Meredith CORPORATION

President and Chief Executive Officer STEPHEN M. LACY

Chairman of the Board WILLIAM T. KERR

In Memoriam — E.T. MEREDITH III (1933-2003)

Diabetic Living Holiday Cooking is part of a series published by Meredith Corp., 1716 Locust St., Des Moines, IA 50309-3023.

If you have comments or questions about the editorial material in *Diabetic Living Holiday Cooking*, write to the editor of *Diabetic Living* magazine, Meredith Corp., 1716 Locust St., Des Moines, IA 50309-3023. Send an e-mail to diabeticliving@meredith.com. *Diabetic Living* magazine is available by subscription or on the newsstand. To order a subscription to *Diabetic Living* magazine, go to DiabeticLivingOnline.com.

contents

Pictured above: **Oven-Fried Chicken Breasts,** and **Macaroni and Cheese**, recipes, page 58

celebration menus

Brussels Sprouts with Toasted Almonds

Putting together a menu for the holidays or a special family meal? No problem! Here we've gathered several menus for any time of the season from a holiday feast, a special dinner for two, or something a little more casual. Take the pressure off and plan your meals with ease.

Brussels Sprouts with Toasted Almonds

These skillet-browned Brussels sprouts are a tasty accompaniment for all types of holiday main dishes including roast beef, pork, or lamb as well as turkey or chicken.

PER SERVING: 86 cal., 6 g total fat (2 g sat. fat), 5 mg chol., 160 mg sodium, 7 g carb., 3 g fiber, 4 g pro. Exchanges: 1 vegetable, 1 fat. Carb choices: 0.5.

2   **pounds fresh Brussels sprouts**
2   **tablespoons olive oil**
1   **14-ounce can reduced-sodium chicken broth**
2   **tablespoons butter**
¾   **teaspoon ground black pepper**
¼   **teaspoon salt**
⅓   **cup sliced almonds, toasted***

1. Trim stems and remove any wilted outer leaves from Brussels sprouts; wash sprouts. Halve Brussels sprouts. In a very large skillet, heat oil over medium heat. Add Brussels sprouts; cook for 6 to 8 minutes or until golden brown, stirring occasionally.

2. Add broth to sprouts. Bring to boiling; reduce heat. Cover and simmer for 5 minutes. Uncover and continue to simmer about 10 minutes more or until most of the liquid has evaporated and the sprouts are tender, stirring occasionally. Add butter, pepper, and salt, stirring until sprouts are coated. Gently stir in toasted sliced almonds. Serve warm. Makes 12 (about ½-cup) servings.

*Test Kitchen Tip: You can toast the almonds in advance and store them in a resealable plastic bag until needed. To toast nuts, preheat oven to 350°F. Spread nuts in a shallow baking pan. Bake, uncovered, for 5 to 10 minutes or until toasted, stirring once or twice. Store at room temperature for up to 1 week or freeze for up to 3 months.

Traditional Roast Turkey

A medley of herbs and vegetables give this golden roasted bird for a crowd fresh-from-the-garden flavor.

PER SERVING: 229 cal., 7 g total fat (2 g sat. fat), 137 mg chol., 155 mg sodium, 0 g carb., 0 g fiber, 38 g pro. Exchanges: 5 very lean meat, 1 fat. Carb choices: 0.

- 1 **12- to 14-pound turkey**
- 1 **tablespoon snipped fresh rosemary or 1 teaspoon dried rosemary, crushed**
- 1 **tablespoon snipped fresh thyme or 1 teaspoon dried thyme, crushed**
- 1 **tablespoon snipped fresh sage or 1 teaspoon dried sage, crushed**
- 1 **teaspoon kosher salt or ½ teaspoon regular salt**
- ½ **teaspoon ground black pepper**
- 3 **small onions, quartered (12 ounces total)**
- 3 **medium carrots, peeled and cut into 2-inch chunks**
- 3 **stalks celery, trimmed and cut into 2-inch chunks**
- 1 **tablespoon olive oil**
  Fresh rosemary sprigs, fresh sage leaves, pomegranate wedges, tiny apples or pears, and/or kumquats (optional)

1. Preheat oven to 425°F. Remove neck and giblets from turkey, reserving neck bone. Rinse the inside of the turkey; pat dry with paper towels. In a small bowl, stir together snipped or dried rosemary, thyme, snipped or dried sage, salt, and pepper. Season inside of body cavity with half of the herb mixture. Pull neck skin to the back; fasten with a skewer. Tuck ends of the drumsticks under the band of skin across the tail. If there is no band of skin, tie the drumsticks securely to the tail with 100-percent-cotton kitchen string. Twist wing tips under the back.

2. Place turkey, breast side up, on a rack in a shallow roasting pan. Arrange onions, carrots, celery, and neck bone around turkey in roasting pan. Pour 1 cup *water* into the pan. Brush turkey with oil. Sprinkle turkey with remaining herb mixture. Insert an oven-going meat thermometer into the center of an inside thigh muscle; the thermometer should not touch bone. Cover turkey loosely with foil.

3. Roast for 30 minutes. Reduce oven temperature to 325°F. Roast for 2½ to 3 hours more or until the thermometer registers 180°F. About 45 minutes before end of roasting, remove foil and cut band of skin or string between drumsticks so thighs cook evenly. When turkey is done, the juices should run clear and the drumsticks should move easily in their sockets.

4. Remove turkey from oven. Transfer to a serving platter (reserve mixture in pan for gravy). Cover; let stand for 15 to 20 minutes before carving. If desired, garnish platter with rosemary sprigs, sage leaves, pomegranate wedges, tiny apples or pears, and/or kumquats. Makes 24 (about 4-ounce) servings.

Turkey Pan Gravy

Straining the liquid from the turkey roasting pan and skimming the gravy keeps the fat in check.

PER SERVING: 18 cal., 0 g total fat (0 g sat. fat), 0 mg chol., 215 mg sodium, 3 g carb., 0 g fiber, 1 g pro. Exchanges: Free. Carb choices: 0.

  Nonstick cooking spray
- 1 **medium onion, peeled and halved horizontally**
  Reduced-sodium chicken broth
- 1 **tablespoon snipped fresh rosemary or 1 teaspoon dried rosemary, crushed**
- 1 **tablespoon snipped fresh sage or 1 teaspoon dried sage, crushed**
- 1 **tablespoon snipped fresh thyme or 1 teaspoon dried thyme, crushed**
- 1 **bay leaf**
- 1 **teaspoon whole black peppercorns**
- ⅓ **cup all-purpose flour**
- ¼ **teaspoon salt**
- ⅛ **teaspoon ground black pepper**

1. Lightly coat an unheated large nonstick skillet with cooking spray. Preheat over medium heat. Add onion to skillet, cut sides down. Cook for 5 to 10 minutes or until onion is charred. Remove from heat; set aside.

2. Strain liquid from turkey roasting pan through a fine-mesh sieve into a 4-cup heatproof glass measure; discard solids. Skim off and discard all of the fat from the liquid. Add enough chicken broth to remaining liquid to measure 3 cups total liquid.

3. Add broth mixture, rosemary, sage, thyme, bay leaf, and black peppercorns to onion halves in skillet. Bring to boiling; reduce heat. Simmer, uncovered, for 7 minutes. Strain broth mixture, discarding solids; return broth mixture to skillet.

4. In a small bowl, combine ½ cup reduced-sodium chicken broth, the flour, salt, and ground black pepper, whisking until smooth. Add to broth in skillet. Cook and stir over medium heat until thickened and bubbly. Cook and stir for 1 minute more. Makes about 3 cups gravy (twelve ¼-cup servings).

Holiday Turkey Menu

Traditional
Roast Turkey

Roasted Root Vegetables

(a potluck holiday)

Planning a turkey potluck? Use these handy tips:

1. **Assign guests** a food category (salad, bread, etc.) or ask a guest to bring a specific dish to ensure variety.

2. **Remember** the two-hour rule. Foods containing meat, poultry, or eggs should be served within two hours of the time they leave the oven, stove top, or refrigerator. Remind guests of that guide.

3. **Clean out** your refrigerator if you are hosting the dinner; you'll need the space.

4. **Plan to prepare** the turkey and gravy if you are the host. Transporting a big bird can be too difficult.

5. **Be considerate** of the host's ability to store the foods you are bringing if you aren't the host.

6. **Keep cold foods** you are toting to the potluck chilled by covering them and packing them in an insulated cooler with ice packs.

7. **Put hot foods** into an insulated casserole carrier. To serve, remove the hot tile and place it under the dish to keep the food hot longer.

8. **Wrap food** in several layers of newspapers and place it in a box if you don't have an insulated carrier. Stuff the corners with crumpled paper to prevent spills.

9. **Use your slow cooker.** You can cook, transport, and serve foods in the same container.

10. **Carry potluck foods** in disposable containers or clearly label your containers, lids, and serving pieces.

Roasted Root Vegetables

Fingerling potatoes are long, narrow baby white potatoes about the size of your finger. Look for them in large supermarkets or farmers' markets.

PER SERVING: 82 cal., 2 g total fat (0 g sat. fat), 0 mg chol., 136 mg sodium, 14 g carb., 3 g fiber, 2 g pro. Exchanges: 1 vegetable, 0.5 starch, 0.5 fat. Carb choices: 1.

12 ounces rutabaga, peeled and cut into ¾-inch pieces (about 3 cups)
8 ounces celery root, peeled and cut into 1-inch pieces (about 2 cups)
8 ounces whole baby carrots with tops (tops trimmed), or 8 ounces packaged peeled baby carrots (1½ cups)
8 ounces fingerling potatoes, halved if large
3 medium parsnips, peeled and cut into 1-inch-thick slices (about 1½ cups)
1 medium fennel bulb, cored and cut into thin wedges (about 1 cup)
2 shallots, peeled and cut into thin wedges (1 cup)
2 tablespoons olive oil
½ teaspoon salt
½ teaspoon ground black pepper

1. Preheat oven to 325°F. In a shallow roasting pan, combine rutabaga, celery root, carrots, potatoes, parsnips, fennel, and shallots. Add oil, salt, and pepper; toss vegetables to coat.

2. Bake, uncovered, for 1 hour, stirring occasionally. Increase oven temperature to 425°F. Bake, uncovered, about 10 minutes more or until vegetables are tender and lightly browned. Makes 12 (½-cup) servings.

Tangerine-Cranberry Relish

The natural sweetness of tangerines means you need less sugar to balance the tartness of cranberries.

PER SERVING: 37 cal., 0 g total fat (0 g sat. fat), 0 mg chol., 1 mg sodium, 10 g carb., 2 g fiber, 0 g pro. Exchanges: 0.5 other carb. Carb choices: 1.
PER SERVING WITH SUBSTITUTE: same as above, except 20 cal., 6 g carb.

1 12-ounce package fresh cranberries (3 cups)
2 medium tangerines
¼ to ⅓ cup sugar or sugar substitute* equivalent to ¼ to ⅓ cup sugar

1. Rinse cranberries under running water and discard any soft or old berries; set aside. Slice each unpeeled tangerine into fifths; remove seeds. Place tangerine slices in a food processor; cover and process until coarsely chopped. Transfer to a medium bowl.

2. Add all but ½ cup of the cranberries to the food processor; cover and process until coarsely chopped. Add to tangerines in bowl; stir in the remaining ½ cup cranberries. Stir in enough of the sugar to sweeten to taste; cover and chill for 1 hour. Stir before serving. Makes 3 cups (twelve ¼-cup servings).

*Sugar Substitutes: Choose from Splenda granular, Equal Spoonful or packets, or Sweet'N Low bulk or packets. Follow package directions to use product amount equivalent to ¼ to ⅓ cup sugar.

Make-Ahead Directions: Prepare as directed. Cover and chill for up to 2 days. Stir before serving.

Tangerine-Cranberry Relish

No-Bake Pumpkin Cheesecake

No-Bake Pumpkin Cheesecake

Pomegranate seeds are a festive garnish
for this flavorful dessert.

PER SERVING: 150 cal., 8 g total fat (4 g sat. fat), 11 mg chol., 144 mg
sodium, 14 g carb., 1 g fiber, 5 g pro. Exchanges: 1 other carb., 1.5 fat.
Carb choices: 1.
PER SERVING WITH SUBSTITUTE: same as above, except 136 cal.,
11 g carb.

1 recipe **Graham Cracker Crust (see recipe, below)**
1 envelope **unflavored gelatin**
¼ cup **water**
1½ 8-ounce tubs **light cream cheese**
1 15-ounce can **pumpkin**
2 tablespoons **sugar or sugar substitute***
   equivalent to 2 tablespoons sugar
1 teaspoon **ground cinnamon**
¾ of an 8-ounce container **frozen light whipped dessert**
   topping, thawed
   Frozen light whipped dessert topping, thawed
   (optional)
   Ground cinnamon, chopped pecans, and/or
   pomegranate seeds (optional)

1. Prepare Graham Cracker Crust; set aside. In a
small saucepan, stir together gelatin and the water; let
stand for 5 minutes to soften. Cook and stir over low heat
until gelatin dissolves; set aside to cool slightly.

2. In a large bowl, beat cream cheese with an electric
mixer on medium speed until smooth. Add pumpkin,
sugar, the 1 teaspoon cinnamon, and the gelatin mixture;
beat until well mixed. Fold in the three-quarters container
of dessert topping. Spread mixture into crust in
springform pan. Cover and refrigerate for 4 to 24 hours
or until set.

3. Using a thin metal spatula or knife, loosen cheesecake
from the side of the springform pan. If desired, use a
wide spatula to remove cheesecake from bottom of pan
and place on a serving plate. Cut into wedges to serve.
If desired, top with additional whipped topping. If desired,
garnish with additional cinnamon, chopped pecans,
and/or pomegranate seeds. Makes 14 servings.

Graham Cracker Crust: Preheat oven to 350°F. In a small
bowl, combine ¾ cup finely crushed graham crackers,
3 tablespoons canola oil, and 2 tablespoons sugar or
sugar substitute* equivalent to 2 tablespoons sugar. Mix
well. Spread evenly in bottom of an 8- or 9-inch
springform pan; press firmly onto bottom. Bake for
5 minutes. Cool on a wire rack.

*Sugar Substitutes: Choose from Splenda granular,
Equal Spoonful or packets, or Sweet'N Low bulk or
packets. Follow package directions to use product
amount equivalent to 2 tablespoons sugar for both crust
and filling.

**Test Kitchen Tip: To remove the seeds from a
pomegranate, cut the pomegranate in half through the
skin. Remove the peel and break the fruit into sections.
Then separate the seeds from the membrane.

Whole Wheat Dressing

Another time, team this versatile dressing with grilled or
roasted beef, pork, or fish.

PER SERVING: 81 cal., 2 g total fat (0 g sat. fat), 0 mg chol., 220 mg sodium,
13 g carb., 2 g fiber, 3 g pro. Exchanges: 1 starch. Carb choices: 1.

10 ounces **whole wheat bread (8 to 10 slices)**
1 tablespoon **olive oil**
1 cup **thinly sliced onion**
1 cup **sliced celery**
1 14-ounce can **reduced-sodium chicken broth**
¼ cup **refrigerated or frozen egg product, thawed, or**
   1 egg, lightly beaten
4 teaspoons **poultry seasoning**
1 tablespoon **snipped fresh parsley**
   Snipped fresh parsley (optional)

1. Preheat oven to 300°F. Cut bread into ½-inch cubes.
Spread cubes in 15×10×1-inch baking pan. Bake for 10 to
15 minutes or until cubes are dry. Cubes will continue to
crisp as they cool. (Or let bread cubes stand, loosely
covered, at room temperature for 8 to 12 hours.) You
should have about 6 cups dried bread cubes. Increase
oven temperature to 325°F.

2. In a large saucepan, heat oil over medium heat.
Add onion and celery. Cook for 5 to 10 minutes or until
tender, stirring occasionally. Remove from heat.

3. Add broth to onion mixture. Stir in egg, poultry
seasoning, and the 1 tablespoon parsley. Add bread
cubes; toss gently to coat. Spoon mixture into a lightly
greased 1½-quart casserole.

4. Bake, uncovered, in the 325°F oven about 45 minutes
or until stuffing is heated through and top is browned.
If desired, garnish with additional parsley. Makes
12 (about ½-cup) servings.

Test Kitchen Tip: The dried bread cubes can be stored
in an airtight container at room temperature for up to
1 day.

Beef & Vegetable Supper

Beef Sirloin with
Oven-Roasted Vegetables
(opposite)

Salad Greens with
Mango-Basil Vinaigrette
(opposite)

Nuts-About-Cranberries Tart
(page 110)

**Beef Sirloin with
Oven-Roasted Vegetables**

Salad Greens with Mango-Basil Vinaigrette

Beef Sirloin with Oven-Roasted Vegetables

Roasting the vegetables along with the beef gives them a toasty herb flavor.

PER SERVING: 265 cal., 9 g total fat (2 g sat. fat), 53 mg chol., 186 mg sodium, 19 g carb., 3 g fiber, 27 g pro. Exchanges: 1 vegetable, 1 starch, 3 lean meat, 0.5 fat. Carb choices: 1.

- 4 teaspoons snipped fresh rosemary or 1 teaspoon dried rosemary, crushed
- 6 cloves garlic, minced
- 1 teaspoon ground black pepper
- ½ teaspoon salt
- 1 3-pound boneless beef top sirloin steak, cut 2 inches thick
- 3 tablespoons olive oil
- 2 pounds small red potatoes
- 12 ounces baby carrots with tops, tops trimmed, or 4 large carrots, halved lengthwise and quartered crosswise
- 2 medium onions, cut into 1-inch-thick wedges
- 3 medium zucchini, cut into 1-inch-thick slices

1. Preheat oven to 425°F. In a small bowl, combine rosemary, garlic, pepper, and salt. Sprinkle 1½ teaspoons of the rosemary mixture evenly onto beef steak; press onto steak with your fingers. Stir oil into the remaining rosemary mixture; set aside.

2. Cut small potatoes in half and any large potatoes into quarters. In a large bowl, combine potatoes, carrots, onions, and the oil-rosemary mixture; toss to coat. Arrange vegetables in a single layer in a shallow baking pan; set aside.

3. Place steak on rack in a separate shallow roasting pan. Insert oven-going meat thermometer so tip is centered in thickest part of steak, not resting in fat. Do not add water or cover. Roast steak and vegetables for 25 minutes. Stir vegetables; add zucchini to baking pan. Roast for 20 to 25 minutes more or until vegetables are tender and meat thermometer registers 140°F for medium-rare doneness.

4. Transfer to a carving board. Cover tightly with foil; let stand for 10 minutes. The temperature after standing should be 145°F for medium-rare doneness.

5. Thinly slice steak. Serve steak with vegetables. Makes 12 servings.

Salad Greens with Mango-Basil Vinaigrette

Fresh and light tasting, this fruity tossed salad will contrast nicely with the heartier dishes in your holiday meal.

PER SERVING: 69 cal., 3 g total fat (1 g sat. fat), 5 mg chol., 127 mg sodium, 9 g carb., 1 g fiber, 2 g pro. Exchanges: 1 vegetable, 0.5 fruit. Carb choices: 0.5.

- 2 24-ounce jars refrigerated mango slices, drained
- ½ cup light red wine vinaigrette salad dressing
- 4 teaspoons snipped fresh basil
- 2 teaspoons snipped fresh mint
- ¼ to ½ teaspoon crushed red pepper
- 12 cups torn mixed salad greens (5 ounces)
- 2 ounces Manchego cheese or Parmesan cheese, finely shredded (½ cup)

1. For mango-basil vinaigrette: Place 1 cup of the mango in a food processor or blender. Cover and process or blend until smooth. Add salad dressing, basil, mint, and crushed red pepper; cover and process or blend just until mixed. Let vinaigrette stand for 5 minutes for flavors to develop.

2. Divide greens evenly among 12 salad plates. Top greens with the remaining mango, breaking mango into bite-size pieces. Drizzle each plate with 2 tablespoons of the mango-basil vinaigrette. Top with cheese. Serve immediately. Makes 12 servings (1 cup greens, about 3 tablespoons mango, 2 tablespoons vinaigrette, and 2 teaspoons cheese).

Herbed Turkey Breast Gala

**Herb-Roasted Turkey
and Vegetables**

Wild Rice Stuffing

2. Place turkey breast portion, bone side down, on a roasting rack in a shallow roasting pan. Lightly coat with cooking spray. Sprinkle the remaining herb mixture evenly over turkey breast; rub in with your fingers. Roast, uncovered, for 20 minutes.

3. Meanwhile, in a large bowl, combine potatoes, carrots, and pearl onions; add reserved 1 tablespoon herb mixture and the olive oil; toss until vegetables are coated. Arrange vegetables around turkey in pan.

4. Reduce oven temperature to 350°F. Roast for 1 1/4 to 1 1/2 hours more or until juices run clear, turkey is no longer pink (170°F), and vegetables are tender, stirring vegetables once.

5. Transfer turkey to cutting board; tent with foil. Let stand for 10 minutes; trim meat from bone. Makes 6 servings (4 ounces meat and 3/4 -cup vegetables each).

Herb-Roasted Turkey and Vegetables

Potatoes, onion, and carrots roast alongside the turkey for an easy side dish.

PER SERVING: 253 cal., 3 g total fat (1 g sat. fat), 75 mg chol., 240 mg sodium, 23 g carb., 4 g fiber, 32 g pro. Exchanges: 1 starch, 3.5 very lean meat, 1 vegetable, 0.5 fat. Carb choices: 1.5.

  2 tablespoons snipped fresh parsley
  4 cloves garlic, minced
  1 teaspoon snipped fresh rosemary
  1 teaspoon snipped fresh thyme
  1/2 teaspoon salt
  1/2 teaspoon ground black pepper
  1 2 3/4- to 3 1/4-pound turkey breast portion with bone, skin removed
     Nonstick cooking spray
  3 cups tiny red potatoes, quartered (about 1 pound)
  2 cups baby carrots with tops trimmed and halved lengthwise (about 8 ounces)
  2 cups white and/or red pearl onions trimmed and halved (about 8 ounces)
  1 tablespoon olive oil

1. Preheat oven to 400°F. In a small bowl, combine parsley, garlic, rosemary, thyme, salt, and pepper. Set aside 1 tablespoon of the herb mixture.

Wild Rice Stuffing

Wild rice adds a nutty flavor to this low-fat dish.

PER SERVING: 79 cal., 1 g total fat (0 g sat. fat), 0 mg chol., 186 mg sodium, 16 g carb., 1 g fiber, 4 g pro. Exchanges: 0.5 starch, 2 vegetable. Carb choices: 1.

  1/4 cup wild rice
  1 3/4 cups water
  1/4 cup regular brown rice
  1 teaspoon instant chicken bouillon granules
  1/8 to 1/4 teaspoon ground sage or nutmeg
  2 cups sliced fresh mushrooms
  1/2 cup sliced celery
  3 green onions, sliced
  1/4 cup sliced almonds or pine nuts, toasted (optional)

1. Rinse uncooked wild rice in a strainer under cold water about 1 minute. In a medium saucepan, combine wild rice, the 1 3/4 cups water, uncooked brown rice, bouillon granules, and sage or nutmeg. Bring to boiling; reduce heat. Cover and simmer for 20 minutes.

2. Add mushrooms, celery, and green onions. Cook, covered, over medium-low heat for 25 minutes more or until vegetables are just tender, stirring frequently. If desired, stir in almonds or pine nuts. Serve immediately or use to stuff a 31/2- to 4-pound broiler-fryer chicken. Makes 5 (1/2-cup) servings.

Make-Ahead Directions: Place stuffing into a 1-quart casserole and chill for up to 24 hours. Stir in 1/4 cup water. Bake, covered, in a 375°F oven about 30 minutes or until heated through.

A fat separator is
a kitchen gadget that
takes the work out of
skimming fat from sauces,
broths, and gravies.
Made of glass or plastic,
it looks similar to a
measuring cup with a
long spout attached
near the bottom of
the container.

Onion-Thyme Gravy

When you skip the drippings from the turkey to make gravy, you keep the fat to a minimum. This flavorful gravy, made without drippings, can be served with any meat.

PER SERVING: 52 cal., 3 g total fat (1 g sat. fat), 7 mg chol., 244 mg sodium, 6 g carb., 0 g fiber, 1 g pro. Exchanges: 0.5 other carb. Carb choices: 0.5.

- 1 large onion, chopped (1 cup)
- 3 shallots, chopped ($\frac{2}{3}$ cup)
- 1 teaspoon snipped fresh thyme or $\frac{1}{4}$ teaspoon dried thyme, crushed
- 2 tablespoons butter
- 2 tablespoons all-purpose flour
- 1 14-ounce can reduced-sodium chicken broth
- 1 tablespoon reduced-sodium soy sauce
- 1 tablespoon Worcestershire sauce
- $\frac{1}{8}$ teaspoon salt
- $\frac{1}{4}$ teaspoon freshly ground black pepper

1. In a medium saucepan, cook onion, shallots, and thyme in hot butter over medium-high heat for 10 to 12 minutes or until vegetables are tender and browned, stirring occasionally.

2. Stir in flour; cook and stir for 1 minute. Add broth, soy sauce, and Worcestershire sauce. Cook and stir until mixture comes to boiling; reduce heat to medium. Simmer, uncovered, for 8 to 9 minutes or until slightly thickened. Stir in the salt and pepper. Serve with Herb-Roasted Turkey and Vegetables. Makes 9 ($\frac{1}{4}$-cup) servings.

Lemony Green Beans

Lemon, garlic, and shallot add lots of flavor to these simple but sophisticated green beans.

PER SERVING: 80 cal., 5 g total fat (1 g sat. fat), 0 mg chol., 152 mg sodium, 9 g carb., 3 g fiber, 2 g pro. Exchanges: 2 vegetable, 1 fat. Carb choices: 0.5.

- 1$\frac{1}{2}$ pound green beans, trimmed, or three 9-ounce packages frozen whole green beans
- 3 tablespoon olive oil
- 3 large shallots, cut into thin wedges
- 6 cloves garlic, thinly sliced
- 1 tablespoon finely shredded lemon peel
- $\frac{1}{2}$ teaspoon salt
- $\frac{1}{8}$ teaspoon ground black pepper
  Lemon wedges

1. In a 12-inch skillet, cook beans in lightly salted boiling water for 2 to 5 minutes or until barely crisp-tender. Drain; rinse beans with cold water. Set aside.

2. In same skillet, heat oil over medium-high heat. Add shallots and garlic. Cook, stirring occasionally, for 2 to 3 minutes or until softened and beginning to brown. Add green beans. Toss for 1 to 2 minutes or until heated through. Remove from heat. Stir in lemon peel, salt, and pepper. Serve green beans with lemon wedges. Makes 8 ($\frac{2}{3}$-cup) servings.

Make-Ahead Tip: Two hours ahead, cook beans as directed in Step 1; cover and chill beans. Thirty minutes ahead, finish recipe as directed in Step 2.

(fresh is best)

Fresh herbs add flavor that can't be matched by dried herbs. If you don't have an herb garden or you can't buy them at a farmer's market, most herbs are available at larger supermarkets. You can keep the herbs fresh for up to 1 week by cutting ½ inch from the stems and standing them, stems submerged and tops covered with a loose-fitting bag, in a jar of water in your refrigerator. The exception is fresh basil, which may blacken in the refrigerator; instead, store it in the same way, but do not refrigerate. Wash and dry the herbs and use kitchen scissors to snip them.

Lemony Green Beans

Pork Loin Dinner

Boneless Pork Loin Roast with
Herbed Pepper Rub
·····················○·····················
Stuffed Onions
(opposite)
·····················○·····················
Fruit with Cider Sauce
(opposite)

Boneless Pork Loin Roast with Herbed Pepper Rub

This Cajun-style recipe is perfect for New Year's Day, when Southerners eat ham and black-eyed peas for luck.

PER SERVING: 242 cal., 6 g total fat (2 g sat. fat), 63 mg chol., 528 mg sodium, 15 g carb., 4 g fiber, 30 g pro. Exchanges: 1 starch, 3.5 lean meat. Carb choices: 1.

- **2 tablespoons grated Parmesan cheese**
- **1 to 2 tablespoons cracked black pepper**
- **2 teaspoons dried basil, crushed**
- **2 teaspoons dried rosemary, crushed**
- **2 teaspoons dried thyme, crushed**
- **¼ teaspoon salt***
- **¼ teaspoon garlic powder**
- **1 3-pound boneless pork top loin roast (single loin)***
- **1 recipe Black-Eyed Pea Salsa (see recipe, right)**

1. Preheat oven to 350°F. For rub, in a small bowl, combine cheese, pepper, basil, rosemary, dried thyme, salt, and garlic powder.

2. Trim fat from pork roast. Pat dry with paper towels. On a sheet of waxed paper, sprinkle rub in an even layer. Roll pork roast in rub to coat on all sides. Place on a rack in a shallow roasting pan. Insert an oven-going meat thermometer into center of roast. Roast for 1¼ to 1½ hours or until thermometer registers 150°F.

3. Cover roast with foil; let stand for 15 minutes. The temperature of the meat after standing should be 160°F. Serve meat with cold or hot Black-Eyed Pea Salsa; garnish with lemon wedges and/or fresh thyme. Makes 12 servings.

Black-Eyed Pea Salsa: In a medium bowl, stir together 2 rinsed and drained 15-ounce cans black-eyed peas; one 16-ounce jar hot, medium, or mild salsa; ½ cup sliced green onions; and ½ teaspoon cracked pepper. Cover and chill until serving time. (Or, if desired, place Black-Eyed Pea Salsa in a medium saucepan; bring just to boiling over medium heat.)

*Test Kitchen Tip: If using enhanced pork in this recipe, omit the salt.

Fruit with Cider Sauce

Count on this medley of pineapple, grapefruit, kiwifruit, and jicama chilled in spiced cider to add a refreshing note to your holiday feast.

PER SERVING: 93 cal., 0 g total fat (0 g sat. fat), 0 mg chol., 4 mg sodium, 23 g carb., 2 g fiber, 1 g pro. Exchanges: 1.5 fruit. 1.5. Carb. choices: 1.5.

¾ cup apple cider or apple juice
2½ inches stick cinnamon
1 20-ounce can pineapple chunks (juice pack), drained
1 large grapefruit, peeled, sectioned, and seeded
3 kiwifruits, peeled and cut into ¼-inch-thick slices
1 cup bite-size sticks peeled jicama

1. In a small saucepan, combine apple cider and stick cinnamon. Bring to boiling; reduce heat. Gently boil, uncovered, about 8 minutes or until reduced to ½ cup liquid. Remove from heat and cool for 10 minutes. Discard stick cinnamon.

2. In a serving bowl, combine pineapple, grapefruit, kiwifruits, and jicama. Pour reduced cider over. Gently stir to combine.

3. Cover and chill for 30 minutes to 4 hours before serving. Makes 8 (½-cup) servings.

Stuffed Onions

Stuffed Onions

Tender baked onions make the perfect edible container for the festive whole wheat couscous pilaf.

PER SERVING: 180 cal., 4 g total fat (1 g sat. fat), 0 mg chol., 164 mg sodium, 34 g carb., 5 g fiber, 4 g pro. Exchanges: 1 vegetable, 2 other carb., 0.5 fat. Carb choices: 2.

8 medium white or yellow onions (about 3 pounds)
4 teaspoons olive oil
2 medium green sweet peppers, seeded and coarsely chopped
⅔ cup cooked whole wheat couscous
½ cup dried currants
2 teaspoons tub-style 60 to 70% vegetable oil spread
½ teaspoon salt
¼ teaspoon ground black pepper
¼ teaspoon smoked paprika or paprika
3 tablespoons Balsamic Drizzle (see recipe, below)

1. Preheat oven to 400°F. Peel off and discard outer layer of each onion. Cut a ½-inch-thick slice from the stem end of each onion; coarsely chop the slices and set aside. Trim a small slice off the opposite end of each onion so it can stand upright. Using a melon baller or small scoop, hollow out each onion, leaving a ¼-inch-thick shell. Save onion centers for another use.

2. Place onion shells on a foil-lined baking sheet; brush outsides of onion shells with 2 teaspoons of the olive oil. Roast about 20 minutes or until lightly browned and almost tender. Remove from oven. Reduce oven temperature to 350°F.

3. Meanwhile, in a large skillet, heat the remaining 2 teaspoons oil over medium heat. Add sweet peppers and chopped onions; cook for 3 to 5 minutes or until tender, stirring occasionally. Remove from heat. Stir in couscous, currants, vegetable oil spread, salt, black pepper, and paprika. Divide evenly among onion shells.

4. Bake, uncovered, for 20 to 25 minutes or until onions are tender and heated through. Drizzle with Balsamic Drizzle. Serve warm. Makes 8 servings.

Balsamic Drizzle: In a heavy small saucepan, bring ½ cup balsamic vinegar to boiling; reduce heat. Simmer, uncovered, about 10 minutes or until reduced by half; remove from heat. Stir in 1 tablespoon low-sugar raspberry jam or apricot jam and 1 teaspoon tub-style 60 to 70% vegetable oil spread; keep warm. Store any unused Balsamic Drizzle in an airtight container in the refrigerator for up to 3 days; drizzle over cooked pork or chicken for added flavor. Makes about ⅓ cup.

Surf & Turf Buffet

**Rosemary Roast Leg of Lamb with
Roasted Fingerling Potatoes**

Rosemary
Roast Leg of Lamb

An herb rub gives tender lamb a robust flavor without
adding a lot of calories, fat, or carbohydrates.

PER SERVING: 136 cal., 4 g total fat (1 g sat. fat), 71 mg chol., 218 mg
sodium, 0 g carb., 0 g fiber, 23 g pro. Exchanges: 3 very lean meat,
0.5 fat. Carb choices: 0.

1 **5- to 7-pound whole lamb leg**
2 **teaspoons snipped fresh rosemary**
1 **teaspoon salt**
1 **teaspoon ground black pepper**
3 **cloves garlic, sliced**

1. Preheat oven to 375°F. Trim fat from lamb. Cut small
slits in lamb. In a small bowl, combine rosemary, salt,
and pepper; sprinkle evenly onto meat. Rub in with
fingers; insert garlic into slits.

2. Place lamb, fat side up, on a rack in a shallow roasting
pan. Add 1 cup water to pan. Insert an oven-going meat
thermometer into center, making sure bulb of thermometer
does not touch bone.

3. Roast until desired doneness, allowing $1\frac{1}{2}$ to
$1\frac{3}{4}$ hours for medium-rare doneness (140°F) or 2 to
$2\frac{1}{4}$ hours for medium (155°F). Cover with foil; let stand
for 15 minutes. The temperature of the meat after standing
should be 145°F for medium-rare or 160°F for
medium. Makes 14 (4-ounce) servings.

Mint Pesto

Basil and mint combine for a delicious condiment for lamb.

PER TABLESPOON: 68 cal., 7 g total fat (1 g sat. fat), 0 mg chol.,
84 mg sodium, 2 g carb., 0 g fiber, 2 g pro. Exchanges: 1.5 fat. Carb
choices: 0.

$1\frac{1}{2}$ **cups loosely packed fresh mint**
$1\frac{1}{2}$ **cups loosely packed fresh basil**
$\frac{1}{2}$ **cup pine nuts, toasted (see tip, page 7)**
$\frac{1}{4}$ **cup olive oil**
4 **cloves garlic, quartered**
$\frac{1}{2}$ **teaspoon salt**

1. In a food processor, combine all ingredients. Cover
and process until almost smooth. Serve with lamb, salmon,
or other meats. Makes 14 (1-tablespoon) servings.
Make-Ahead Directions: Prepare as directed. Cover
surface with plastic wrap. Chill up to 24 hours.

Quick Tip

Plan ahead for the big meal.
Order the leg of lamb in
advance. You can store it in
the fridge for up to 5 days.
The Mint Pesto and Herbed
Balsamic Vinaigrette can
be made up to 24 hours in
advance. Toss the salad
ingredients and the fruit
cups a couple of hours
before the meal.

Roasted
Fingerling Potatoes

Add to the oven with the lamb
the last 45 minutes of roasting.

PER SERVING: 93 cal., 2 g total fat (0 g sat. fat), 0 mg chol., 89 mg sodium,
17 g carb., 2 g fiber, 2 g pro. Exchanges: 1 starch, 0.5 fat. Carb choices: 1.

3 **pounds fingerling potatoes or round red potatoes**
2 **tablespoons olive oil**
1 **teaspoon paprika**
$\frac{1}{2}$ **teaspoon salt**
$\frac{1}{4}$ **to $\frac{1}{2}$ teaspoon ground black pepper**

1. Preheat oven to 375°F. Wash potatoes; pat dry. Cut
any larger potatoes into 2-inch pieces.

2. Place potatoes in a large roasting pan; drizzle with
olive oil. Sprinkle with paprika, salt, and pepper; stir
potatoes to coat.

3. Bake, uncovered, about 45 minutes or until potatoes
are tender and brown, stirring occasionally. Makes
14 ($\frac{1}{2}$-cup) servings.

(plank it)

When you want a new way to cook fish (and the weather is cooperating, of course), wood planks for the grill add great flavor to grilled fish. Choose from different types of woods, such as alder, cedar, or maple. Flavored planks—try Cajun or lemon-dill—add even more taste. Each plank is used just once. You'll find them where other barbeque products are sold. Keep them on hand for other foods, too. Try the planks with cheese or vegetables (such as zucchini, onion, or sweet pepper).

**Grilled Salmon
with Lemon Thyme**

Grilled Salmon with Lemon Thyme
Cedar smoke from grill planks and lemon give salmon all the flavor it needs.

PER SERVING: 210 cal., 11 g total fat (3 g sat. fat), 69 mg chol., 171 mg sodium, 0 g carb., 0 g fiber, 26 g pro. Exchanges: 4 very lean meat. Carb choices: 0.

- 2 cedar grill planks (each about 12×6×¾ inches)
- 2 2-pound fresh or frozen salmon fillets (with skin), cut 1 inch thick
- 3 tablespoons olive oil
- 2 teaspoons snipped fresh lemon thyme or ½ teaspoon dried thyme, crushed
- ½ teaspoon salt
- ½ teaspoon ground black pepper
  Fresh lemon thyme sprigs (optional)
- 2 medium lemons, cut into wedges

1. At least 1 hour before grilling, soak planks in enough water to cover, weighing them down to keep them submerged. Thaw salmon, if frozen. Rinse fish; pat dry with paper towels.

2. On each plank, place a fillet, skin side down. Brush oil onto fish. Sprinkle fish with snipped thyme, salt, and pepper.

3. Place salmon on planks on grill rack directly over low heat. Cover and grill about 20 minutes or until salmon flakes easily when tested with a fork.

4. If desired, garnish with lemon thyme sprigs. Serve with lemon wedges. Makes 14 (4-ounce) servings.

Feta-Stuffed Mini Peppers

Feta-Stuffed Mini Peppers

To make ahead, prepare as directed through Step 2. Cover and chill for up to 24 hours. Bake as directed in Step 3.

PER SERVING: 48 cal., 3 g total fat (2 g sat. fat), 14 mg chol., 186 mg sodium, 2 g carb., 1 g fiber, 3 g pro. Exchanges: 0.5 medium-fat meat, 0.5 vegetable. Carb choices: 0.

- 28 **miniature sweet peppers**
- 4 **ounces fresh spinach**
- 8 **ounces feta cheese, crumbled**

1. Preheat oven to 375°F. Cut a thin slice from tops or sides of peppers. Scoop out and discard seeds. If desired, reserve tops.

2. For filling, wash spinach; remove stems. Cut spinach leaves into thin strips. In a large bowl, combine spinach and feta cheese. Spoon filling into pepper shells, mounding slightly. In a 3-quart rectangular baking dish, arrange peppers, stuffed sides up. If desired, add pepper tops.

3. Bake, uncovered, for 18 to 20 minutes or until sweet peppers are slightly soft. Makes 14 servings.

Mixed Greens with Herbed Balsamic Vinaigrette

Try any herb you like in this vinaigrette.

PER SERVING: 76 cal., 6 g total fat (1 g sat. fat), 0 mg chol., 86 mg sodium, 5 g carb., 1 g fiber, 1 g pro. Exchanges: 1 vegetable, 1 fat. Carb choices: 0.

- 1 **pound torn mixed baby greens (mesclun) (about 16 cups)**
- 1 **medium cucumber, halved lengthwise and sliced**
- 4 **plum tomatoes, sliced**
- ¾ **cup pitted kalamata or ripe olives**
- ¼ **cup snipped fresh chives**
- 1 **recipe Herbed Balsamic Vinaigrette (see recipe, below)**

1. In a very large bowl, toss together greens, cucumber, plum tomatoes, olives, and chives. Stir Herbed Balsamic Vinaigrette; pour onto salad. Toss gently to coat. Makes 14 (1-cup) servings.

Herbed Balsamic Vinaigrette: In a food processor or blender, combine ⅓ cup balsamic vinegar, ⅓ cup olive oil, 2 tablespoons fresh oregano, and 2 quartered cloves garlic. Cover and process until mixed. Season to taste with ground black pepper. Makes about ⅔ cup.

Make-Ahead Directions: Prepare vinaigrette; chill for up to 24 hours.

Citrus Fruit Cups

Tangy lime juice and peel add flavor yet almost no calories.

PER SERVING: 49 cal., 0 g total fat (0 g sat. fat), 0 mg chol., 1 mg sodium, 12 g carb., 2 g fiber, 1 g pro. Exchanges: 1 fruit. Carb choices: 1.

- 4 **medium pink grapefruit**
- 3 **medium oranges**
- 3 **medium tangerines**
- 2 **cups fresh strawberries**
- 1 **cup fresh blueberries**
- 2 **kiwifruits, peeled and cut into wedges**
- 2 **medium limes**
  Fresh mint sprigs (optional)

1. Peel and section grapefruit and oranges. Peel tangerines; cut in half lengthwise then slice crosswise. Quarter strawberries.

2. In a large bowl, combine grapefruit, oranges, tangerines, and strawberries. Add blueberries and kiwifruits; toss gently.

3. Finely shred peel from limes to make 1 tablespoon peel. Squeeze juice to make about ¼ cup juice. Gently stir peel and juice into fruit. Cover; chill. To serve, spoon fruit into dessert cups. If desired, garnish each serving with fresh mint sprigs. Makes 14 (½-cup) servings.

Minted French Green Beans

Haricots verts are very thin French green beans, but you can use regular green beans.

PER SERVING: 38 cal., 2 g total fat (0 g sat. fat), 0 mg chol., 140 mg sodium, 4 g carb., 2 g fiber, 1 g pro. Exchanges: 1.5 vegetable. Carb choices: 0.

8 ounces haricots verts or other small, thin green beans (2 cups)
1 tablespoon finely chopped shallot
2 teaspoons extra virgin olive oil
2 teaspoons chopped fresh mint
1 teaspoon lemon juice
  Kosher salt
  Freshly ground black pepper

1. Rinse beans. If desired, trim tips off beans; drain.

2. Place a steamer basket in a large skillet. Add water to just below the bottom of basket. Bring water to boiling. Place beans in steamer basket. Cover and steam for 2 minutes. Drain. Rinse with cold water. (Or plunge into ice water.) Drain well.

3. In a medium bowl, lightly toss together beans, shallot, oil, mint, and lemon juice. Season to taste with salt and pepper. Cover and chill for 2 hours. Makes 4 servings.

A Dazzling Dinner

Balsamic-Glazed Lamb Chops
(opposite)

-------------------○-------------------

Couscous with Zucchini and Cherry Tomatoes (below)

-------------------○-------------------

Minted French Green beans
(at left)

Couscous with Zucchini and Cherry Tomatoes

Whole wheat couscous is not only good for you, it also adds a delightful, nutty flavor to this colorful side dish.

PER SERVING: 134 cal., 1 g total fat (0 g sat. fat), 0 mg chol., 223 mg sodium, 27 g carb., 5 g fiber, 6 g pro. Exchanges: 1.5 starch, 1 vegetable. Carb choices: 2.

1 teaspoon olive oil
1 small onion, thinly sliced and separated into rings
1 clove garlic, minced
1¼ cups reduced-sodium chicken broth
12 ounces zucchini, trimmed, cut crosswise into 3 pieces, and cut lengthwise into ½-inch-thick wedges
2 teaspoons snipped fresh thyme or ½ teaspoon dried thyme, crushed
¼ teaspoon salt
1 cup halved cherry tomatoes
¾ cup whole wheat couscous
  Fresh thyme sprigs (optional)

1. In a large saucepan, heat oil over medium heat. Add onion and garlic; cook about 6 minutes or until tender and golden, stirring occasionally. Add broth; bring onion mixture to boiling.

2. Add zucchini, the 2 teaspoons thyme, and the salt. Cook about 3 minutes or until zucchini is crisp-tender. Stir in tomatoes and couscous. Remove from heat. Cover; let stand about 5 minutes or until broth is absorbed.

3. Fluff with a fork. If desired, garnish with thyme sprigs. Serve warm. Makes 6 (⅔-cup) servings.

Couscous with Zucchini and Cherry Tomatoes

Balsamic-Glazed Lamb Chops

A captivating quartet of orange juice, balsamic vinegar, honey, and soy sauce brings out the best in succulent, low-carb lamb rib chops.

PER SERVING: 161 cal., 6 g total fat (2 g sat. fat), 48 mg chol., 334 mg sodium, 10 g carb., 0 g fiber, 15 g pro. Exchanges: 0.5 other carb., 2.5 lean meat. Carb choices: 0.5.

 8 lamb rib chops, cut 1 inch thick (1½ pounds total)
 ¼ teaspoon salt
 ¼ teaspoon ground black pepper
 ½ cup orange juice
 ¼ cup balsamic vinegar
 1 tablespoon honey
 1 tablespoon reduced-sodium soy sauce

1. Trim fat from chops. Season chops with salt and pepper. Place chops in a resealable plastic bag set in a shallow dish. In a small bowl, stir together orange juice, balsamic vinegar, honey, and soy sauce; pour over chops. Seal bag; turn to coat chops. Marinate in the refrigerator for 4 to 24 hours, turning bag occasionally.

2. Drain lamb, reserving marinade. Pour marinade into a heavy small saucepan. Bring to boiling; reduce heat. Boil gently, uncovered, about 15 minutes or until reduced to about ⅓ cup; set aside.

3. Place chops on the rack of an uncovered grill directly over medium coals. Grill to desired doneness, turning and brushing once with glaze halfway through grilling. (Allow 12 to 14 minutes for medium-rare doneness [145°F] or 15 to 17 minutes for medium doneness [160°F.) Discard any remaining glaze. Makes 4 servings.

(opt for fish)

The American Heart Association recommends eating at least two servings (3 ounces each) of fish weekly to help reduce the risk of heart disease. Diets high in monounsaturated and polyunsaturated fats lower LDL ("bad") cholesterol levels. The polyunsaturated fat category contains two subclasses of fatty acids: omega-6 fatty acids and omega-3 fatty acids. Vegetable oils, such as corn, sunflower, safflower, and soybean, are rich in omega-6 fatty acids. Besides fatty fish, soybean oil is an excellent source of omega-3 fatty acids, as are canola oil and deep-sea fish.

Lemon and Parmesan Fish

Crushed cornflakes add satisfying crunch to these baked fish fillets; lemon peel boosts the flavor.

PER SERVING: 191 cal., 7 g total fat (4 g sat. fat), 71 mg chol., 230 mg sodium, 7 g carb., 0 g fiber, 25 g pro. Exchanges: 0.5 starch, 3 very lean meat, 1 fat. Carb choices: 0.5.

- **4 2-ounce fresh or frozen sole, tilapia, or flounder fillets, ¼ to ½ inch thick**
- **Nonstick cooking spray**
- **¼ cup crushed cornflakes**
- **2 tablespoons grated Parmesan cheese**
- **2 teaspoons butter, melted**
- **½ teaspoon finely shredded lemon peel**
- **⅛ teaspoon ground black pepper**
- **Lemon wedges**

1. Preheat oven to 450°F. Thaw fish, if frozen. Rinse fish; pat dry with paper towels. Lightly coat a shallow baking pan with cooking spray. Roll up fish fillets, starting from the short ends. Place in prepared baking pan.

2. In a small bowl, combine crushed cornflakes, Parmesan cheese, melted butter, lemon peel, and pepper. Sprinkle crumb mixture on top of fish roll-ups; use your fingers to lightly press crumbs into fish. (Some crumbs may fall off fish into pan.)

3. Bake for 6 to 8 minutes or until fish flakes easily when tested with a fork and crumbs are browned. Serve the fish and any crumbs from the baking pan with lemon wedges. Makes 2 servings.

Lemon and Parmesan Fish

Dinner for a Duo

Lemon and Parmesan Fish
(at left)

----------------○----------------

Roasted Asparagus Parmesan
(at right)

----------------○----------------

Fresh Tomato Sauce with Pasta
(below)

Fresh Tomato Sauce with Pasta

Fresh Tomato Sauce with Pasta

Be sure to use the best tomatoes available for the sauce.
During winter, purchase plum, cherry, or grape
tomatoes for the sweetest flavor.

PER SERVING: 202 cal., 6 g total fat (1 g sat. fat), 5 mg chol., 202 mg
sodium, 31 g carb., 2 g fiber, 8 g pro. Exchanges: 2 starch, 1 fat. Carb
choices: 2.

- 2 tablespoons finely chopped onion or shallot
- 1 clove garlic, minced
- 2 teaspoons olive oil
- 2 cups peeled, seeded, and chopped ripe fresh
  tomatoes (about 1½ pounds)
- ⅛ teaspoon salt
- ⅛ teaspoon ground black pepper
- 2 tablespoons sliced pitted ripe olives
- 2 tablespoons snipped fresh basil or 1 teaspoon dried
  basil, crushed
- 3 ounces dried capellini or spaghetti
  Freshly shredded Parmesan cheese

1. For sauce, in a large saucepan, cook onion and
garlic in hot oil until onion is tender but not brown.

2. Stir in 1 cup of the tomatoes, salt, and pepper. Bring
to boiling; reduce heat. Simmer, uncovered, for 15 minutes,
stirring occasionally. Stir in remaining tomatoes, olives,
and basil. Heat through.

3. Meanwhile, cook pasta according to package
directions. Drain. Serve sauce over pasta. Sprinkle with
Parmesan cheese. Makes 3 side-dish servings.

Roasted Asparagus Parmesan

This is an easy dish to make for serving
alongside the lemony fish. It also complements
the tomatoes in the pasta side dish.

PER SERVING: 57 cal., 4 g total fat (1 g sat. fat), 3 mg chol., 65 mg sodium,
2 g carb., 1 g fiber, 3 g pro. Exchanges: 1 vegetable, 1 fat. Carb choices: 0.

- 8 ounces fresh asparagus spears
- 2 teaspoons olive oil
- ⅛ teaspoon salt-free seasoning blend
- 2 tablespoons finely shredded Parmesan cheese

1. Preheat oven to 400°F. Meanwhile, snap off and discard
woody bases from asparagus spears. If desired, scrape
off scales. Place asparagus in a 15×10×1-inch baking pan.
Drizzle with oil, tossing gently to coat. Spread in a single
layer. Sprinkle with seasoning blend.

2. Bake for 12 to 15 minutes or until asparagus is crisp-
tender. Transfer to a serving platter; sprinkle with
Parmesan cheese. Makes 2 side-dish servings.

Go-Fish Dinner

Tilapia with Herbed Shiitake Sauce
(opposite)

Caramelized Onion Risotto
(opposite)

Mascarpone-Stuffed Figs with
Valencia Orange Glaze (page 107)

Tilapia with Herbed Shiitake Sauc
and **Caramelized Onion Risotto**

Tilapia with Herbed Shiitake Sauce

When shopping, look for moist, cleanly cut fillets with a fresh, not fishy, aroma.

PER SERVING: 220 cal., 4 g total fat (1 g sat. fat), 75 mg chol., 369 mg sodium, 11 g carb., 1 g fiber, 32 g pro. Exchanges: 0.5 starch, 4 very lean meat, 1 fat. Carb choices: 1.

6 ½- to ¾-inch-thick fresh or frozen skinless tilapia, pollock, or cod fillets (about 2 pounds total)
Nonstick cooking spray
2 teaspoons lemon juice
¼ cup fine dry bread crumbs
¼ teaspoon salt
¼ to ½ teaspoon ground black pepper
1 recipe Herbed Shiitake Sauce (see recipe, below)
Fresh thyme sprigs (optional)
Lemon slices (optional)

1. Thaw fish, if frozen. Preheat oven to 450°F. Lightly coat a shallow baking pan with cooking spray; set aside.

2. Rinse fish; pat dry with paper towels. Brush fish with lemon juice. Arrange fish fillets, skin sides down, in the prepared baking pan. For coating, in a small bowl, combine bread crumbs, salt, and pepper. Sprinkle the crumb coating evenly onto the top sides of fish. Coat fish generously with spray.

3. Measure the thickness of the fish. Bake fish, crumb sides up, until the flesh flakes easily when tested with a fork. (Allow 4 to 6 minutes per ½-inch thickness of fish.) Do not turn the fish during baking.

4. Serve fish with Herbed Shiitake Sauce. If desired, garnish each serving with thyme sprigs and lemon slices. Makes 6 servings.

Herbed Shiitake Sauce: In a large skillet, heat 2 teaspoons olive oil over medium-high heat. Add 1½ cups sliced shiitake mushrooms and 2 tablespoons finely chopped shallots or sweet onion. Cook, uncovered, about 3 minutes or until mushrooms are tender, stirring occasionally.

Stir in 1 tablespoon all-purpose flour. Stir in ½ cup dry white wine or reduced-sodium chicken broth; cook and stir until thickened and bubbly. Add ¾ cup reduced-sodium chicken broth. Bring to boiling; reduce heat. Simmer, uncovered, for 4 minutes, stirring often.

Stir in 1 tablespoon snipped fresh chives, 1 tablespoon snipped fresh parsley, and 2 teaspoons snipped fresh thyme or ½ teaspoon crushed dried thyme. Heat through. Serve sauce with fish. Makes about 1½ cups sauce.

Quick Tip

When making the risotto, alternately adding the hot stock and rice allows the rice to absorb the liquid yet retain its shape and produce a creamy consistency. Any kind of long grain rice will work, but Italian cooks prefer Arborio rice.

Caramelized Onion Risotto

Browning the onions slowly adds a toasted caramel flavor to the rice. Your guests will be pleasantly surprised.

PER SERVING: 106 cal., 3 g total fat (1 g sat. fat), 4 mg chol., 227 mg sodium, 17 g carb., 0 g fiber, 4 g pro. Exchanges: 1 starch, 0.5 fat. Carb choices: 1.

1 14-ounce can reduced-sodium chicken broth
2 teaspoons olive oil
1 cup chopped onion
2 cloves garlic, minced
¾ cup Arborio rice
⅓ cup grated Parmesan cheese
¼ teaspoon ground white pepper

1. In a medium saucepan, combine chicken broth and 1½ cups *water;* heat over high heat until hot but not boiling. Reduce heat to low and keep warm.

2. Meanwhile, in a large skillet, heat oil over medium heat. Add onion; cook about 10 minutes or until onion is brown and tender. Add garlic; cook and stir for 1 minute.

3. Carefully add ½ cup of the broth mixture to onion mixture, stirring to loosen brown bits in the skillet. Bring to boiling; reduce heat. Simmer, uncovered, about 4 minutes or until the liquid is reduced by half.

4. Add uncooked rice and ½ cup of the broth mixture. Cook and stir for 3 to 4 minutes or until the rice has absorbed the liquid. Continue adding the hot broth mixture, ½ cup at a time, cooking until all of the liquid has been absorbed before adding more, stirring often.

5. When the rice is fully cooked but still slightly firm in the center, remove the skillet from the heat. Stir in the Parmesan cheese and white pepper. Serve warm. Makes 6 (⅓-cup) servings.

Red Bean Lasagna

Low-fat cheeses and egg product make this meatless lasagna perfect for a healthful meal.

PER SERVING: 243 cal., 6 g total fat (2 g sat. fat), 13 mg chol., 631 mg sodium, 29 g carb., 6 g fiber, 18 g pro. Exchanges: 1.5 starch, 2 lean meat, 1 vegetable. Carb choices: 2.

- 1 tablespoon cooking oil
- 1 large onion, chopped (1 cup)
- 1 medium carrot, chopped (½ cup)
- 1 clove garlic, minced
- 1 15- to 16-ounce can red beans, rinsed and drained
- 1 14½-ounce can diced tomatoes, undrained
- ¼ cup snipped fresh parsley
- 1 tablespoon snipped fresh basil or 1½ teaspoons dried basil, crushed
- 2 teaspoons snipped fresh oregano or 1 teaspoon dried oregano, crushed
- 6 dried whole wheat or regular lasagna noodles
- 2 cups sliced fresh mushrooms
- 1 12-ounce carton low-fat cottage cheese, drained
- 1 cup shredded part-skim mozzarella cheese (4 ounces)
- ¼ cup refrigerated or frozen egg product, thawed, or 1 egg, lightly beaten
- ¼ cup grated **Parmesan** cheese
- 3 cups coarsely chopped fresh spinach
- 2 tablespoons coarsely snipped fresh parsley, basil, and/or oregano (optional)

Red Bean Lasagna

1. In a large skillet, heat oil over medium heat. Add onion, carrot, and garlic. Cook for 5 minutes or until just tender, stirring occasionally. Add beans, undrained tomatoes, the ¼ cup parsley, the 1 tablespoon basil, and the 2 teaspoons oregano. Bring to boiling; reduce heat. Simmer, covered, for 15 minutes.

2. Meanwhile, cook lasagna noodles according to package directions; drain and rinse with cold water. Drain again.

3. Preheat oven to 375°F. With a potato masher, mash bean mixture slightly in skillet. Add mushrooms to skillet; simmer, uncovered, for 15 minutes more, stirring occasionally. Meanwhile, in a medium bowl, combine cottage cheese, ½ cup of the mozzarella cheese, the egg, and Parmesan cheese; set aside.

4. Spread ½ cup of the bean mixture in a 2-quart rectangular baking dish. Arrange two noodles in a single layer on top of the bean mixture. Spread with one-third of the cheese mixture. Top evenly with one-third of the remaining bean mixture. Top with half of the spinach. Repeat layers twice, starting with noodles and ending with bean mixture.

5. Bake, covered, for 40 minutes or until heated through. Top with remaining mozzarella cheese. Bake, uncovered, 5 minutes more or until cheese is melted. Let stand for 10 minutes before serving. If desired, top with the 2 tablespoons fresh parsley, basil, and/or oregano. Makes 8 servings.

Roasted Balsamic Vegetables

This vegetable side adds color to any plate. Balsamic vinegar adds a subtle sweetness.

PER SERVING: 90 cal., 4 g total fat (1 g sat. fat), 0 mg chol., 45 mg sodium, 13 g carb., 3 g fiber, 2 g pro. Exchanges: 2 vegetable, 1 fat. Carb choices: 1.

- 1 **pound green beans, ends trimmed (if desired)**
- 1 **medium red onion, cut into thin wedges**
- 2 **cloves garlic, minced**
- 2 **tablespoons olive oil**
- ⅛ **teaspoon salt**
- ⅛ **teaspoon ground black pepper**
- 4 **medium yellow summer squash, halved lengthwise and sliced ¼ inch thick**
- ⅔ **cup balsamic vinegar**

1. Preheat oven to 450°F.
2. In a shallow roasting pan, combine beans, onion, and garlic. Drizzle vegetables with olive oil; sprinkle

---

Meatless Medley

Red Bean Lasagna
(opposite)

-----------------○-----------------

Roasted Balsamic Vegetables
(at left)

-----------------○-----------------

Nutty Cheese-Topped Figs
(page 108)

---

with salt and pepper. Toss mixture until beans are evenly coated. Spread into a single layer on bottom of pan.

3. Roast vegetables for 8 minutes. Stir in squash; roast for 5 to 7 minutes more or until vegetables are tender and lightly browned.

4. Meanwhile, in a small saucepan, bring balsamic vinegar to boiling over medium-high heat; reduce heat. Boil gently for 8 to 10 minutes or until vinegar is reduced by half (vinegar will thicken slightly).

5. Drizzle vinegar over roasted vegetables; toss until vegetables are evenly coated. Makes 8 to 10 servings.

Roasted Balsamic Vegetables

A Southern Dinner

Cheddar Shrimp and Grits
(below)

Collard Greens
(at right)

Baked Tomatoes and Okra
(opposite)

She-Crab Soup (page 36)

Peanut Butter and Vanilla Custards
(page 36)

Cheddar Shrimp and Grits

This savory recipe features two Carolina Low Country
essentials: shrimp and grits.

PER SERVING: 274 cal., 6 g total fat (2 g sat. fat), 152 mg chol., 384 mg
sodium, 30 g carb., 2 g fiber, 27 g pro. Exchanges: 2 starch, 3 very lean
meat. Carb choices: 2.

- 1¼ **pounds fresh or frozen medium shrimp in shells**
- 1 **14-ounce can reduced-sodium chicken broth**
- 1½ **cups fat-free milk**
- 1 **cup regular grits**
- 2 **teaspoons olive oil**
- 1 **large onion, thinly sliced into rings**
- 2 **cloves garlic, minced**
- 1 **tablespoon snipped fresh parsley**
- ½ **cup shredded reduced-fat cheddar cheese (2 ounces)**
- ¼ **cup sliced green onions**

1. Thaw shrimp, if frozen. Peel and devein shrimp,
leaving tails intact if desired; set aside. In a medium
saucepan, combine broth, milk, and grits. Bring to boiling;
reduce heat. Cover and simmer for 4 to 5 minutes or until
grits are desired consistency, stirring occasionally.

2. In a large skillet, heat oil over medium heat. Add onion
and garlic; cook and stir about 5 minutes or until onion is
tender and lightly browned. Remove mixture from skillet;
set aside. Add shrimp to hot skillet; cook over medium heat
for 2 to 4 minutes or until shrimp are opaque, turning
occasionally. Stir in onion mixture and parsley.

3. Divide grits among six bowls; top with shrimp.
Sprinkle with cheese and green onions. Makes
6 (1-cup) servings.

Collard Greens

Collard greens are a type of cabbage.
Shop for bright green bunches with no brown spots.

PER SERVING: 39 cal., 1 g total fat (0 g sat. fat), 0 mg chol., 137 mg sodium,
6 g carb., 3 g fiber, 2 g pro. Exchanges: 1 vegetable. Carb choices: 0.5.

- 2 **pounds fresh collard greens**
- 1 **teaspoon olive oil**
- 1 **medium onion, sliced and separated into rings**
- 1 **14-ounce can reduced-sodium chicken broth**
- 1 **smoked turkey neck bone or smoked turkey
  drumstick bone***
- ¼ **teaspoon ground black pepper**

1. Wash collard greens thoroughly. Cut off stems and
discard. Coarsely chop collard greens and set aside. (You
should have about 9 cups packed.) In a 4-quart Dutch
oven, heat olive oil over medium heat. Add onion; cook
about 5 minutes or until tender.

2. Add collard greens, chicken broth, smoked turkey
bone, and pepper. Bring to boiling; reduce heat. Cover
and simmer about 1 hour or until collard greens are
tender. Remove smoked turkey bone and drain off any
excess liquid. Serve warm with a slotted spoon. Makes
6 (about ⅓-cup) servings.

*Test Kitchen Tip: If using a turkey drumstick, remove
meat and reserve for another use; use only the bone for
this recipe.

Collard Greens and
Cheddar Shrimp and Grits

Baked Tomatoes and Okra

Tomatoes and okra are a traditional Southern combo. This updated version includes lima beans and the zip of crushed red pepper.

PER SERVING: 55 cal., 0 g total fat (0 g sat. fat), 0 mg chol., 112 mg sodium, 12 g carb., 3 g fiber, 3 g pro. Exchanges: 2 vegetable. Carb choices: 1.

½ cup loose-pack frozen lima beans

8 ounces fresh okra, washed, stemmed, and cut into ½-inch-thick slices, or 2 cups frozen cut okra, thawed

4 medium tomatoes, chopped

1 medium onion, sliced and separated into rings

½ of a medium yellow or green sweet pepper, seeded and cut into thin strips

¼ to ½ teaspoon crushed red pepper

¼ teaspoon salt

1. Preheat oven to 350°F. Cook lima beans according to package directions; drain. In a 2-quart casserole, combine lima beans, okra, tomatoes, onion, sweet pepper, crushed red pepper, and salt.

2. Bake, covered, for 45 minutes; stir. Bake, uncovered, for 30 minutes more; stir. Serve with a slotted spoon. Makes 6 (⅔-cup) servings.

She-Crab Soup

This Carolina favorite is usually made with crab roe. Red caviar, a tasty substitute, is available year-round .

PER SERVING: 160 cal., 3 g total fat (0.5 g sat. fat), 39 mg chol., 579 mg sodium, 19 g carb., 1 g fiber, 9 g pro. Exchanges: 1 starch, 1 very lean meat, 0.5 fat. Carb choices: 1.

- 1 tablespoon olive oil
- 1 cup chopped onion
- ½ cup sliced celery
- 2 cloves garlic, minced
- ⅓ cup dry sherry
- ½ cup brown rice
- 1 recipe Fish Stock (see recipe, right) or 3 cups reduced-sodium chicken broth
- 2 tablespoons crab roe or red caviar
- 2 cups fat-free half-and-half
- 8 ounces fresh or frozen cooked crabmeat, cartilage removed and flaked*
- 1 tablespoon snipped fresh chives

1. In a large saucepan, heat olive oil over medium-high heat; add onion, celery, and garlic. Cook and stir until tender. Add sherry. Bring to a boil; reduce heat. Boil gently, uncovered, until liquid is nearly evaporated.

2. Stir in uncooked brown rice. Add Fish Stock and crab roe. Bring to boiling; reduce heat. Cover and simmer about 40 minutes or until rice is very tender. Cool mixture slightly.

3. In a blender, puree rice mixture, half at a time if necessary, until almost smooth. Return to saucepan; stir in half-and-half. Heat through. Stir in crabmeat. Sprinkle individual servings with snipped chives. Makes 8 (¾-cup) servings.

Fish Stock: Place the shells from 1 pound large shrimp in a large saucepan. Add 1 medium carrot, chopped; 1 stalk celery with leaves, chopped; 1 small onion, chopped; 3 sprigs fresh parsley; 1 bay leaf; 3 whole black peppercorns; and ½ teaspoon salt. Add 3½ cups water and 1 tablespoon lemon juice. Bring to boiling; reduce heat. Cover and simmer for 45 minutes. Strain through 100-percent-cotton cheesecloth; discard solids. Store stock in the refrigerator for up to 3 days or in the freezer for up to 6 months. Makes about 3 cups.

*Test Kitchen Tip: You can substitute canned lump crabmeat if fresh or frozen is not available.

Peanut Butter and Vanilla Custards

Smooth and creamy, these two-tone desserts feature reduced-fat peanut butter and fat-free half-and-half.

PER SERVING: 171 cal., 6 g total fat (1 g sat. fat), 0 mg chol., 172 mg sodium, 21 g carb., 1 g fiber, 7 g pro. Exchanges: 1.5 other carb., 0.5 high-fat meat. Carb choices: 1.5.

PER SERVING WITH SUGAR SUBSTITUTE: same as above, except 142 cal., 14 g carb. Exchanges: 1 other carb. Carb choices: 1.

- 2 cups fat-free half-and-half
- ¼ cup sugar or sugar substitute* equivalent to ¼ cup sugar
- 1 envelope unflavored gelatin
- ¼ cup reduced-fat creamy peanut butter
- ½ teaspoon vanilla
- 2 tablespoons dry-roasted peanuts, chopped

1. In a medium saucepan, combine half-and-half, sugar, and gelatin. Let stand for 5 minutes. Cook and stir over medium heat until gelatin is dissolved. Remove from heat. Add peanut butter and vanilla. Whisk until smooth. Pour into six 6-ounce custard cups. Cover; chill about 3 hours or until set (mixture will separate into layers).

2. To serve, loosen edges and unmold custards onto individual dessert plates. Sprinkle with peanuts. Makes 6 (¾-cup) servings.

*Sugar Substitutes: Choose from Splenda granular or Sweet'N Low bulk or packets. Follow package directions to use product amount equivalent to ¼ cup sugar.

She-Crab Soup

Peanut Butter and
Vanilla Custards

(half-and-half without the half?)

Half-and-half has always been something you could feel a little better about using in place of whipping cream because it is lower in fat and calories. A relatively new product is fat-free half-and-half. Although the name is a bit perplexing and a little confusing, fat-free half-and-half is made mostly of fat-free (skim) milk. It can be used in place of regular half-and-half in most cooking and baking applications. Because it is similar to fat-free milk, you save a lot of fat and calories if you use a substantial amount to substitute for regular half-and-half (120 calories and 3 g fat for fat-free versus 315 calories and 28 g fat for regular half-and-half per cup).

Grilled Peppered Pork Chops with Mediterranean Relish

The easy-to-make relish adds bright color and sun-kissed Italian and Greek flavors to the pork.

PER SERVING: 215 cal., 6 g total fat (1 g sat. fat), 83 mg chol., 390 mg sodium, 6 g carb., 1 g fiber, 35 g pro. Exchanges: 1 vegetable, 4 lean meat. Carb choices: 0.5.

- **6 boneless pork top loin chops, cut ¾-inch thick (about 2 pounds total)**
- **1 6½-ounce jar marinated artichoke hearts**
- **1 teaspoon bottled hot pepper sauce**
- **1½ cups chopped tomatoes**
- **½ cup bottled roasted red sweet peppers, drained and chopped**
- **¼ cup pitted ripe olives, sliced**
- **1 small fresh jalapeño chile pepper, seeded and finely chopped (optional) (see tip, page 53)**
- **Fresh oregano sprigs (optional)**

1. Place chops in large resealable plastic bag. Drain artichokes, reserving marinade. Add hot pepper sauce to reserved marinade; pour over chops. Seal bag; turn to coat chops. Place bag in a shallow dish. Marinate in the refrigerator for 15 to 30 minutes.

2. For relish, coarsely chop artichoke hearts. In a medium bowl, combine artichokes, tomatoes, roasted red peppers, olives, and, if desired, chile pepper.

3. Drain chops, discarding marinade. Place chops on rack of an uncovered grill directly over medium coals. Grill for 7 to 9 minutes or until chops are slightly pink in the center and juices run clear (160°F), turning once halfway through grilling.

4. Serve chops with relish. If desired, garnish with oregano. Makes 6 servings.

Pork Chop Supper

Grilled Peppered Pork Chops with Mediterranean Relish
(at left)

-------------------○-------------------

Fennel Corn Bread Stuffing
(opposite)

-------------------○-------------------

Green Beans and Onions
(opposite)

Grilled Peppered Pork Chops with Mediterranean Relish

Fennel Corn Bread Stuffing

Who needs a bird? This stuffing bakes in a casserole, reducing fat and calories from turkey or chicken juices.

PER SERVING: 172 cal., 6 g total fat (0 g sat. fat), 0 mg chol., 256 mg sodium, 24 g carb., 1 g fiber, 4 g pro. Exchanges: 1.5 starch, 1 fat. Carb choices: 1.5.

Nonstick cooking spray
1 8.5-ounce package corn muffin mix
½ cup refrigerated or frozen egg product, thawed
⅓ cup fat-free milk
2 tablespoons olive oil
1 medium fennel bulb, trimmed, cored, and thinly sliced
1 medium kohlrabi, peeled and finely chopped
1 clove garlic, minced
½ cup water
1 teaspoon poultry seasoning
¼ teaspoon ground black pepper

1. Preheat oven to 400°F. Lightly coat an 8×8×2-inch baking pan with cooking spray; set aside. In a medium bowl, combine corn muffin mix, ¼ cup of the egg, and the milk; stir just until moistened (batter should be lumpy). Pour into prepared pan, spreading evenly. Bake for 20 to 25 minutes or until a toothpick inserted in center comes out clean. Cool completely in pan on a wire rack.

2. Lightly coat a 2-quart square baking dish with cooking spray; set aside. In a large skillet, heat 1 tablespoon of the oil over medium-high heat. Add fennel, kohlrabi, and garlic; cook for 5 to 7 minutes or until vegetables are tender, stirring frequently. If vegetables begin to overbrown, reduce heat. Transfer vegetables to a very large bowl.

3. Preheat oven to 375°F. Cut up corn bread and add to vegetables. In a small bowl, combine the remaining ¼ cup egg, the remaining 1 tablespoon oil, the water, poultry seasoning, and pepper. Pour egg mixture over corn bread mixture. Stir until well mixed.

4. Transfer corn bread mixture to prepared baking dish. Bake, uncovered, about 20 minutes or until heated through. Makes 8 (about ⅔-cup) servings.

Green Beans and Onions

Green Beans and Onions

Green beans take on an exciting new flavor from onion, roasted red peppers, olives, and a sweet, tangy sauce.

PER SERVING: 73 cal., 3 g total fat (0 g sat. fat), 0 mg chol., 153 mg sodium, 11 g carb., 4 g fiber, 2 g pro. Exchanges: 1.5 vegetable, 0.5 fat. Carb choices: 1.

1 tablespoon olive oil
1½ cups chopped onion
1 tablespoon balsamic vinegar or red wine vinegar
½ cup bottled roasted red sweet peppers, drained and chopped
¼ cup sliced pitted ripe olives
2 tablespoons snipped fresh basil or 1½ teaspoons dried basil, crushed
¼ teaspoon salt
⅛ teaspoon ground black pepper
1 pound fresh green beans, trimmed and cut into 2-inch-long pieces

1. In a large nonstick skillet, heat oil over medium-low heat. Add onion; cook about 10 minutes or until onion is very tender and golden brown. Stir in vinegar. Cook and stir for 1 to 2 minutes more or until liquid is evaporated. Stir in roasted red peppers, olives, basil, salt, and black pepper. Remove from heat; cover and keep warm.

2. Meanwhile, in a covered large saucepan, cook green beans in a small amount of boiling water about 10 minutes or until crisp-tender; drain. Stir the onion mixture into green beans. Makes 6 (½-cup) servings.

Grilled Snapper with Red Pepper Sauce

For a two-color sauce, prepare half a recipe with yellow sweet pepper and half a recipe with red sweet pepper, then swirl them on the plate.

PER SERVING: 194 cal., 8 g total fat (1 g sat. fat), 41 mg chol., 223 mg sodium, 4 g carb., 1 g fiber, 26 g pro. Exchanges: 3.5 very lean meat, 1 vegetable, 1.5 fat. Carb choices: 0.5.

- 2 tablespoons olive oil
- 4 4- to 6-ounce fresh or frozen skinless red snapper fillets
- 1 large red sweet pepper, seeded and chopped
- 2 medium tomatoes, peeled, seeded, and chopped
- 2 tablespoons white wine vinegar
- ¼ teaspoon salt
-    Dash cayenne pepper
- 1 tablespoon fresh snipped basil or oregano or ½ teaspoon dried basil or oregano, crushed
-    Red and/or yellow cherry tomatoes (optional)
-    Fresh basil or oregano sprigs (optional)

1. Thaw fish, if frozen. Rinse fish and pat dry with paper towels. Measure thickness of fish.

2. For red pepper sauce, in a small skillet, heat 1 tablespoon of the oil over medium heat. Add sweet pepper; cook for 3 to 5 minutes or until tender, stirring occasionally. Stir in tomatoes, 1 tablespoon of the vinegar, the salt, and cayenne pepper. Cook about 5 minutes or until tomatoes soften, stirring occasionally. Cool slightly. Transfer mixture to a blender or food processor. Cover and blend or process until smooth. Return sauce to skillet; keep warm over low heat.

3. In a small bowl, stir together the remaining 1 tablespoon vinegar, remaining 1 tablespoon oil, and the snipped or dried basil; brush onto snapper fillets.

4. Place fish on the lightly greased rack of an uncovered grill directly over medium coals. Grill for 4 to 6 minutes per ½-inch thickness of fish or until fish flakes easily when tested with a fork, turning fish once halfway through grilling.

5. Serve fish with red pepper sauce. If desired, garnish with cherry tomatoes and fresh basil sprigs. Makes 4 servings.

Dinner with Friends

Grilled Snapper with
Red Pepper Sauce
(at left)

-----------------○-----------------

Zucchini alla Roma
(below)

-----------------○-----------------

Brown Rice Pilaf
(at right)

Zucchini alla Roma

Traditional Italian flavors such as garlic and olive oil
combine with zucchini and dried herb
for a simple but tasty side dish.

PER SERVING: 40 cal., 3 g total fat (1 g sat. fat), 2 mg chol., 125 mg sodium, 3 g carb., 1 g fiber, 2 g pro. Exchanges: 1 vegetable, 0.5 fat. Carb choices: 0.

- 1 tablespoon olive oil
- 2 cloves garlic, minced
- 4 small zucchini, sliced (4 cups)
- 1 teaspoon dried mint or dried basil, crushed, or
  1 tablespoon snipped fresh mint or basil
- ¼ teaspoon salt
  Dash ground black pepper
- 2 tablespoons finely shredded Romano or Parmesan cheese

1. In a large skillet, heat oil over medium heat. Add garlic; cook for 30 seconds.

2. Add zucchini, dried mint or basil (if using), salt, and pepper to oil in skillet. Cook, uncovered, over medium heat about 5 minutes or until zucchini is crisp-tender, stirring occasionally.

3. To serve, sprinkle with Romano cheese and fresh mint or basil (if using). Makes 6 servings.

Brown Rice Pilaf

Green onions and marjoram flavor nutty brown rice for a
side that complements both fish and meat entrées.

PER SERVING: 60 cal., 1 g total fat (0 g sat. fat), 0 mg chol., 230 mg sodium, 13 g carb., 2 g fiber, 2 g pro. Exchanges: 0.5 starch, 0.5 vegetable. Carb choices: 1.

- 1 cup water
- 1 teaspoon instant chicken bouillon granules
- 1 cup sliced fresh mushrooms
- ¾ cup instant brown rice
- ½ cup shredded carrot
- ¾ teaspoon snipped fresh marjoram or ¼ teaspoon dried marjoram, crushed
  Dash ground black pepper
- ¼ cup thinly sliced green onions
- 1 tablespoon snipped fresh parsley

1. In a medium saucepan, stir together water and bouillon granules. Bring to boiling. Stir in mushrooms, uncooked rice, carrot, marjoram, and pepper. Return to boiling; reduce heat. Simmer, covered, for 12 minutes.

2. Remove from heat. Let stand, covered, for 5 minutes. Add green onions and parsley; toss gently with a fork. Makes 4 (¾-cup) servings.

**Brown
Rice Pilaf**

Cheddar and Zucchini Frittata

This Italian-style egg dish is great for brunch,
but also try it for a light supper another time.

PER SERVING: 115 cal., 5 g total fat (2 g sat. fat), 10 mg chol., 321 mg
sodium, 6 g carb., 1 g fiber, 11 g pro. Exchanges: 1.5 lean meat,
0.5 vegetable, 0.5 fat. Carb choices: 0.5.

- **1   cup refrigerated or frozen egg product, thawed, or
    4 eggs**
- **½ cup finely shredded reduced-fat cheddar cheese**
- **2   tablespoons snipped fresh flat-leaf parsley**
- **¼ teaspoon ground black pepper**
- **⅛ teaspoon salt**
- **2   teaspoons olive oil**
- **12 ounces zucchini, halved lengthwise and sliced**
- **4   green onions, sliced**

1. Position a rack in the upper third of the oven and
preheat to 450°F. In a medium bowl, whisk together eggs,
cheese, half of the parsley, the pepper, and salt. Set egg
mixture aside.

2. In a 9- to 10-inch ovenproof skillet, heat olive oil over
medium-high heat. Add zucchini and green onions; cook
5 to 8 minutes or just until tender, stirring frequently.

3. Carefully pour the egg mixture over the vegetables.
Reduce heat to medium. As mixture sets, run a spatula
around the edge of the skillet, lifting egg mixture so
uncooked portion flows underneath. Continue cooking
and lifting edges about 5 minutes or until egg mixture is
almost set (surface will be moist). Reduce heat as
necessary to prevent overbrowning.

4. Place the skillet in the oven. Bake about 5 minutes
or until the frittata is firm and the top is golden. Sprinkle
with remaining 2 tablespoons parsley. Serve warm. Cut
into wedges. Makes 4 servings.

**Cheddar and
Zucchini Frittata**

Marinated Orange Slices

These delicate honey-sweetened oranges
are a nice not-too-sweet addition to this brunch menu.
You can also serve them as a dessert.

PER SERVING: 202 cal., 6 g total fat (1 g sat. fat), 82 mg chol.,
229 mg sodium, 2 g carb., 0 g fiber, 34 g pro. Exchanges: 4.5 very lean
meat, 1 fat. Carb choices: 0.

- **¾ cup pomegranate juice**
- **1   tablespoon honey**
- **3   oranges, peeled and thinly sliced crosswise**

- **12 pitted dates, snipped (about ⅓ cup)**
- **3   tablespoons coarsely chopped, lightly salted dry-
    roasted pistachio nuts**
- **3   tablespoon pomegranate seeds (optional)**
- **1½ ounces Parmesan or Manchego cheese, thinly
    shaved (optional)**

1. In a small bowl, combine pomegranate juice and
honey. Add orange slices, tossing gently to coat. Cover
and chill for at least 2 hours or up to 24 hours, tossing
slices occasionally.

2. Drain orange slices, discarding marinade. Place
in a serving bowl or on serving plates. Top with dates,
pistachio nuts, and, if desired, pomegranate seeds. If
desired, top with cheese. Makes 6 servings.

Brunch Menu

Marinated
Orange Slices

Savory Brunch Strudel

Wrapped in a flaky crust, this ham-and-cheese strudel with asparagus is elegant and delicious.

PER SERVING: 142 cal., 2 g fat (1 g sat. fat), 68 mg chol., 271 mg sodium, 3 g carb., 1 g fiber, 28 g pro. Exchanges: 0.5 vegetable, 4 very lean meat. Carb choices: 0.

- 1 cup fat-free or light ricotta cheese
- ¼ cup freshly shredded **Asiago** or **Parmesan cheese**
- 1 ounce chopped lower-fat cooked ham
- 1 2-ounce jar diced pimiento, drained
- 2 tablespoons thinly sliced green onion
- 2 tablespoons snipped fresh dill or 1 teaspoon dried dillweed
- 1 egg white, lightly beaten
- ¼ teaspoon salt
- ¼ teaspoon ground black pepper
- 8 ounces asparagus, cut into ½-inch pieces, or ½ of a 10-ounce package frozen cut asparagus
- Butter-flavor nonstick spray coating
- 10 sheets frozen phyllo dough, thawed
- ¼ cup fine dry bread crumbs

1. For filling, in a large bowl, combine ricotta cheese, Asiago cheese, ham, pimiento, green onion, dill, egg white, salt, and pepper.

2. In a covered small saucepan, cook the asparagus in a small amount of boiling water for 4 to 5 minutes or just until crisp-tender (don't overcook). Drain. Rinse with cold water; drain. Stir into the ricotta mixture.

3. Lightly coat a large baking sheet with cooking spray; set baking sheet aside. Place 1 sheet of phyllo on a dry kitchen towel (keep remaining phyllo covered with a damp kitchen towel to prevent drying out). Lightly coat with cooking spray. Top with another sheet of phyllo. Lightly coat with cooking spray. Sprinkle with one-fourth of the bread crumbs. Repeat with remaining phyllo and remaining bread crumbs. Lightly coat the last layer with cooking spray.

4. Spoon the filling lengthwise onto half of the top layer of phyllo, leaving about a 1½-inch border on all sides. Fold in the short sides over filling. Starting from a long side, roll up into a spiral.

5. Place strudel, seam side down, on the prepared baking sheet. Spray top of strudel with cooking spray. Using a sharp knife, score into 12 slices, cutting through the top layer only. If desired, sprinkle with additional bread crumbs.

6. Bake in a 375°F oven about 30 minutes or until light brown. Let stand for 10 minutes before serving. To serve, cut along scored lines into slices. Makes 6 servings.

Apricot Ladder Loaf

This recipe makes two loaves (12 servings per loaf). If you don't need both loaves, use only half of the bread dough and make bread rolls with the other half.

PER SERVING: 54 cal., 0 g total fat (0 g sat. fat), 0 mg chol., 6 mg sodium, 10 g carb., 0 g fiber, 1 g pro. Exchanges: 1 other carb. Carb choices: 1.

- Nonstick cooking spray
- 1 16-ounce loaf frozen white or whole wheat bread dough, thawed*
- ½ cup sugar-free apricot, strawberry, or red raspberry spread
- ½ cup chopped apricots; chopped, peeled peaches; blueberries; or raspberries

1. Preheat oven to 350°F. Lightly coat 2 baking sheets with cooking spray; set aside. Transfer thawed dough onto a lightly floured surface. Divide dough in half. Roll each half of dough into a 12×7-inch rectangle. Carefully transfer each rectangle to a prepared baking sheet.

2. Cut up any large pieces of fruit in the preserves. For each loaf, spoon about ¼ cup of the preserves down the center third of the dough rectangle to within 1 inch of the ends. Sprinkle ¼ cup of the fruit over the preserves. On the long sides, make 2-inch-long cuts from the edges toward the center at 1-inch intervals. Starting at one end, alternately fold opposite strips of dough, at an angle, across filling. Slightly press the ends together in the center to seal. Cover and let rise in a warm place until nearly double (about 40 minutes).

3. Bake about 20 minutes or until golden brown. Remove from baking sheets. Cool slightly on wire racks; serve warm. Makes 2 loaves (24 servings).

*Test Kitchen Tip: To quick-thaw frozen bread dough in your microwave oven, remove bread dough from wrapper and place it in a microwave-safe bowl. Cover and cook on 10 percent power (low) for 15 to 17 minutes or until thawed, rotating the dough frequently.

Apricot Ladder Loaf

(hold the eggs)

When feasible, substitute refrigerated or frozen egg product for eggs in recipes such as cookies, cakes, brownies, and bar cookies. Use ¼ cup egg product for each whole egg. Avoid using egg product in recipes where egg whites are beaten with sugar, such as those for angel food cakes or meringues. Egg substitute will save you about 215 mg cholesterol, 5 grams fat, and 45 calories per ¼ cup (the equivalent of one large egg).

Green Bean Salad

A Casual Affair

Greek-Style Turkey Burgers
(at right)

Green Bean Salad
(below)

Chocolate Chip Pumpkin Bars
(page 109)

Green Bean Salad

Cooking in the microwave oven makes prep fast and easy.

PER SERVING: 96 cal., 7 g total fat (1 g sat. fat), 0 mg chol., 134 mg sodium, 8 g carb., 4 g fiber, 2 g pro. Exchanges: 2 vegetable, 1 fat. Carb choices: 0.5.

 12 **ounces fresh green beans, trimmed**
 ⅓ **cup fresh parsley, coarsely chopped**
 4 **green onions, sliced**
 2 **stalks celery, chopped**
 2 **tablespoons olive oil**
 2 **tablespoons lime juice**
  Salt
  Ground black pepper
  Lime wedges (optional)

1. In a 2-quart microwave-safe dish add green beans and 2 tablespoons *water*. Cover and microwave on 100 percent power (high) for 5 minutes or until tender, stirring halfway. Drain; rinse with cold water and drain again. Transfer to serving dish. Toss with parsley, green onions, celery, oil, and juice. Cover and let stand at room temperature for up to 30 minutes.

2. To serve, sprinkle salad with salt and pepper; if desired, squeeze lime wedges over salad. Makes 4 to 6 (¾-cup) servings.

Greek-Style Turkey Burgers

These lean, juicy burgers bask in mellow Greek flavor from feta cheese, olives, and cucumber.

PER SERVING: 278 cal., 9 g total fat (3 g sat. fat), 26 mg chol., 379 mg sodium, 39 g carb., 2 g fiber, 13 g pro. Exchanges: 2 starch, 0.5 lean meat, 1.5 vegetable, 1 fat. Carb choices: 2.5

 ⅓ **cup fine dry whole wheat bread crumbs***
 1 **egg white, lightly beaten**
 1 **tablespoon plain low-fat yogurt**
 1 **teaspoon snipped fresh rosemary or ½ teaspoon dried rosemary, crushed**
 1 **teaspoon snipped fresh oregano or ½ teaspoon dried oregano, crushed**
 1 **tablespoon crumbled feta cheese**
 ⅛ **teaspoon ground black pepper**
 1 **pound uncooked ground turkey breast or chicken breast**
  Mixed torn greens (optional)
 1 **recipe Olive-Tomato Salsa (see recipe, opposite)**
 ¼ **cup crumbled feta cheese (1 ounce)**
  Plain low-fat yogurt (optional)
 2 **whole wheat pita bread rounds, halved and lightly toasted**

46 DIABETIC LIVING | **HOLIDAY COOKING**

1. In a medium bowl, combine bread crumbs, egg white, the 1 tablespoon yogurt, the rosemary, oregano, 1 tablespoon feta cheese, and the pepper. Add ground turkey; mix well. Shape turkey mixture into four ³⁄₄-inch-thick patties.

2. Place patties on the greased rack of an uncovered grill directly over medium coals. Grill for 12 to 14 minutes or until no longer pink (165°F),** turning patties once halfway through grilling.

3. If desired, divide greens among four serving plates; top with burgers. Top burgers with Olive-Tomato Salsa, the ¹⁄₄ cup feta cheese, and, if desired, additional yogurt. Serve burgers with pita bread. Makes 4 servings.

Olive-Tomato Salsa: In a small bowl, stir together 1 cup chopped, seeded tomatoes; ¹⁄₄ cup chopped, seeded cucumber; ¹⁄₄ cup chopped, pitted kalamata or other ripe olives; ¹⁄₂ teaspoon snipped fresh rosemary or ¹⁄₄ teaspoon dried rosemary, crushed; and ¹⁄₂ teaspoon snipped fresh oregano or ¹⁄₄ teaspoon dried oregano, crushed. Makes about 1¹⁄₂ cups.

*__Test Kitchen Tip:__ For fine dry whole wheat bread crumbs: Place 1 slice whole wheat bread, toasted, in a food processor. Cover and process until fine crumbs form. Measure ¹⁄₃ cup.

**__Test Kitchen Tip:__ The internal color of a burger is not a reliable doneness indicator. A turkey or chicken patty cooked to 165°F is safe, regardless of color. To measure the doneness of a patty, insert an instant-read thermometer through the side of the patty to a depth of 2 to 3 inches.

Greek-Style Turkey Burgers

Carolina Barbecued Pork,
Baked Navy Beans, and
Country Slaw (recipe, page 50)

Carolina Barbecued Pork

Finely chopped pork is traditional in the
Lexington area of the Carolinas, while pulled or
coarsely chopped pork is more popular on the coast.

PER SERVING: 267 cal., 11 g fat (4 g sat. fat), 113 mg chol., 307 mg sodium,
4 g carb., 0 g fiber, 34 g pro. Exchanges: 5 lean meat. Carb choices: 0.

5   or 6 mesquite wood chunks
1   6- to 8-pound boneless pork shoulder roast,
    rolled and tied
1   recipe Sweet 'n' Spicy Rub (see recipe, opposite)
1   recipe Herb Vinegar Basting Sauce
    (see recipe, opposite)

1. At least 1 hour before cooking, soak wood chunks in enough water to cover. Drain before using.

2. Sprinkle roast evenly on all sides with Sweet 'n' Spicy Rub; rub in with your fingers. Center roast on spit rod of rotisserie; secure with holding forks.* Test balance, making adjustments as necessary. Arrange medium coals around a drip pan. Add wood chunks to coals. Attach spit, then turn on the motor and cover grill.

3. Let the roast rotate over the drip pan for 3 to 3¼ hours or until an instant-read thermometer inserted in the center of the roast registers 170°F, brushing occasionally with Herb Vinegar Basting Sauce during the last hour of grilling. Add additional coals and wood chunks as needed to maintain temperature and smoke during grilling.

Carolina BBQ

4. Remove the roast from the spit; wrap in foil. Let rest for 15 minutes. Remove foil and string; remove and discard fat. Chop or shred the pork. Makes 16 to 24 servings.

Sweet 'n' Spicy Rub: In a small bowl, stir together 2 tablespoons packed brown sugar, 2 teaspoons chili powder, 1½ teaspoons kosher salt, 1½ teaspoons garlic powder, 1½ teaspoons onion powder, 1½ teaspoons ground cumin, ¾ teaspoon cayenne pepper, and ¾ teaspoon ground black pepper. Makes about ½ cup.

Herb Vinegar Basting Sauce: In a large saucepan, combine 2 cups cider vinegar, 2 tablespoons tomato paste, 1 tablespoon packed brown sugar, 3 minced cloves garlic, 1 teaspoon poultry seasoning, 1 teaspoon crushed red pepper, ½ teaspoon snipped fresh rosemary, and ½ teaspoon snipped fresh thyme. Bring to boiling; reduce heat. Simmer, uncovered, for 5 minutes. Remove from heat; let cool. Strain liquid; discard solids. Makes 1¾ cups.

*Test Kitchen Tip: If you don't have a rotisserie, you can use a covered charcoal grill or a gas grill.

For the charcoal grill, arrange medium coals around a drip pan. Add wood chunks to coals. Test for medium-low heat above the drip pan. Place the roast on the grill rack over the drip pan. Cover and grill roast for 3 to 3¼ hours or until an instant-read thermometer inserted in the center of the roast registers 170°F, brushing occasionally with Herb Vinegar Basting Sauce during the last hour of grilling. Add additional coals and wood chunks as needed to maintain the temperature and smoke during grilling.

For the gas grill, preheat grill. Reduce heat to medium-low. Adjust for indirect cooking. Grill as above, except place roast on a rack in a roasting pan.

Baked Navy Beans

Start from scratch with dry navy beans to avoid the sodium that's in canned beans.

PER SERVING: 211 cal., 4 g total fat (1 g sat. fat), 0 mg chol., 252 mg sodium, 36 g carb., 10 g fiber, 11 g pro. Exchanges: 2.5 starch, 1 very lean meat. Carb choices: 2.5.

PER SERVING WITH SUBSTITUTE: same as above, except 203 cal., 33 g carb. Exchanges: 2 starch. Carb choices: 2.

- **1 pound dry navy beans**
- **8 cups water**
- **2 cups chopped onions**
- **2 cloves garlic, minced**
- **1 tablespoon olive oil**
- **2 14-ounce cans (3½ cups) reduced-sodium chicken broth**
- **3 cups water**
- **¼ cup molasses**
- **¼ cup ketchup**
- **3 tablespoons peanut butter**
- **2 tablespoons packed brown sugar or brown sugar substitute* equivalent to 2 tablespoons brown sugar**
- **1 tablespoon yellow mustard**
- **1 teaspoon Worcestershire sauce**

1. Rinse beans. In a 4-quart Dutch oven, combine beans and the 8 cups water. Cover; let soak in a cool place for 6 to 8 hours or overnight. (Or bring to boiling; reduce heat. Simmer for 2 minutes. Remove from heat. Cover; let stand for 1 hour.) Rinse and drain beans.

2. In the same Dutch oven, cook onions and garlic in hot oil until tender, stirring occasionally.

3. Add the drained navy beans, chicken broth, and the 3 cups water. Bring to boiling; reduce heat. Cover and simmer over low heat for 1 to 1½ hours or until beans are tender, stirring occasionally during cooking. Drain the beans, reserving the cooking liquid.

4. Meanwhile, preheat oven to 300°F. Return drained beans to the Dutch oven. Stir in 2 cups of the reserved cooking liquid, the molasses, ketchup, peanut butter, brown sugar, mustard, and Worcestershire sauce.

5. Bake, covered, about 2½ hours or until desired consistency, stirring the beans occasionally. Makes 12 (½-cup) servings.

*Sugar Substitutes: Choose from Sweet'N Low Brown or Sugar Twin Granulated Brown. Follow the package directions to use the product amount that's equivalent to 2 tablespoons brown sugar.

Country Slaw

A sweet-and-sour dressing and sweet onions lend fantastic flavor to this homey side salad.

PER SERVING: 45 cal., 0 g total fat (0 g sat. fat), 0 mg chol., 159 mg sodium, 10 g carb., 2 g fiber, 2 g pro. Exchanges: 1 vegetable, 0.5 carb. Carb choices: 0.5.

PER SERVING WITH SUBSTITUTE: same as above, except 33 cal., 8 g carb.

1 recipe Tomato Vinaigrette (see recipe, right)
3 pounds cabbage, cored and cut into small chunks
2 medium carrots, peeled and sliced
1 medium sweet onion (such as Vidalia, Maui, or Walla Walla), cut into chunks

1. Prepare Tomato Vinaigrette; set aside.

2. Place cabbage, carrots, and onion in a food processor. Working in batches, cover and process vegetables until chopped. Transfer vegetables to a very large bowl.

3. Pour the warm vinaigrette onto chopped vegetables; toss gently to coat. Cover and chill for 2 hours. Makes 16 (about ½-cup) servings.

Tomato Vinaigrette: In a small saucepan, combine ¾ cup cider vinegar, ¼ cup sugar or sugar substitute* equivalent to ¼ cup sugar, ¼ cup ketchup, 1 tablespoon Dijon-style mustard, 1½ teaspoons celery seeds, ½ teaspoon salt, and ¼ teaspoon ground black pepper. Bring to boiling; reduce heat. Simmer, uncovered, for 6 to 8 minutes or until liquid is reduced to ¾ cup. (The aroma from the simmering vinegar is potent! Be careful not to breathe too deeply while liquid is steaming.) Remove from heat; cool for 15 minutes.

*Sugar Substitutes: Choose from Splenda granular, Equal Spoonful or packets, or Sweet'N Low bulk or packets. Follow the package directions to use the product amount equivalent to ¼ cup sugar. If using Equal Spoonful or packets, stir the sweetener into the vinaigrette after removing the saucepan from the heat.

Make-Ahead Directions: Prepare the slaw as directed, except cover and chill for up to 8 hours.

Country Slaw

Old-Fashioned Peach Cobbler

Choose a cookie cutter shape to match the holiday or event.

PER SERVING: 175 cal., 4 g fat (3 g sat. fat), 11 mg chol., 129 mg sodium, 34 g carb., 4 g fiber, 3 g pro. Exchanges: 1 fruit, 1 carb., 1 fat. Carb choices: 2.

PER SERVING WITH SUBSTITUTE: same as above, except 147 cal., 28 g carb. Exchanges: 0.5 carb.

- ⅓ cup sugar or sugar substitute* equivalent to ⅓ cup sugar
- 2 tablespoons cornstarch
- ½ teaspoon ground cinnamon
- 10 cups sliced, pitted fresh peaches (3½ to 4 pounds) or 10 cups frozen unsweetened peach slices, thawed
- ½ cup water
- 1¼ cups whole wheat flour
- 2 tablespoons sugar or sugar substitute* equivalent to 2 tablespoons sugar
- ¾ teaspoon baking powder
- ¼ teaspoon baking soda
- ¼ teaspoon salt
- ¼ cup butter
- ½ cup buttermilk
  Vanilla frozen yogurt (optional)

Old-Fashioned Peach Cobbler

1. Preheat oven to 400°F. For filling, in a very large bowl, stir together the ⅓ cup sugar, the cornstarch, and cinnamon. Add the sliced peaches and toss gently to mix. Gently stir in the water. Spread the peach mixture evenly in a 3-quart rectangular baking dish. Set aside.

2. For the whole wheat biscuit star cutouts, in a medium bowl, stir together whole wheat flour, the 2 tablespoons sugar, the baking powder, baking soda, and salt. Using a pastry blender, cut in butter until mixture resembles coarse crumbs. Make a well in the center of the flour mixture. Add buttermilk all at once. Using a fork, stir just until the flour mixture is moistened. Knead the dough gently to shape into a ball.

3. On a lightly floured surface, roll dough to ½-inch thickness. Using a 2- to 2½-inch star cookie cutter, cut out 12 stars, rerolling as needed. Arrange the dough stars on top of the fruit mixture.

4. Bake, uncovered, for 25 to 30 minutes or until the stars are light brown and the peach mixture is bubbly in the center. Cool on a wire rack for 30 minutes. Serve warm. If desired, serve with frozen yogurt. Makes 12 servings (1 star plus about ⅔ cup peach mixture).

*Sugar Substitutes: Choose from Splenda granular or Sweet'N Low bulk or packets. Follow the package directions to use the product amounts equivalent to ⅓ cup and 2 tablespoons sugar.

Make-Ahead Directions: Prepare the biscuit star cutouts as directed in Steps 2 and 3. Cover with plastic wrap and chill for up to 4 hours. Continue to assemble the cobbler as directed in Steps 1 and 4.

Quick Tip

Good old-fasioned fruit cobblers are the ultimate dessert. But what if the fruit you need isn't in season? No problem. Use frozen. You can enjoy this peach cobbler year-round, even if a fresh peach is nowhere in sight.

Beef Flank Steak with Creamy Poblano Chile Sauce

Flank Steak Dinner

Beef Flank Steak with
Creamy Poblano Chile Sauce
(at left)

Corn-on-the-Cob Pudding
(below)

Caramel Apple Crisp
(page 114)

resealable plastic bag. Seal bag; turn to coat steak. Place bag in a large bowl. Marinate in the refrigerator for 6 to 24 hours, turning bag occasionally.

2. For poblano chile sauce, preheat oven to 425°F. Place chile pepper on foil-lined baking sheet. Bake for 20 to 25 minutes or until skin is charred. Wrap in the foil; let stand about 10 minutes or until cool enough to handle. Remove and discard skin, stem, and seeds. In a small nonstick skillet, heat oil over medium-high heat. Add onion and the 1 clove garlic; cook and stir for 3 to 4 minutes or until tender. In a food processor or blender, combine onion mixture, chile pepper, yogurt, sour cream, and the ¼ teaspoon salt. Cover; process or blend until smooth; stir in cilantro. Cover and chill until serving time.

3. Remove steak from marinade; discard marinade. Place steak on rack of an uncovered grill directly over medium coals. Grill for 17 to 21 minutes for medium-rare to medium doneness (145°F to 160°F), turning once. To serve, cut steak across the grain into thin slices; serve with poblano chile sauce. Makes 6 servings.

Beef Flank Steak with Creamy Poblano Chile Sauce

For maximum flavor, tenderize flank steak with the spunky citrus marinade the night before.

PER SERVING: 203 cal., 8 g total fat (3 g sat. fat), 50 mg chol., 216 mg sodium, 5 g carb., 0 g fiber, 26 g pro. Exchanges: 3.5 lean meat. Carb choices: 0.

½ cup lime juice
½ cup orange juice
1 teaspoon ground cumin
2 cloves garlic, minced
½ teaspoon chili powder
1 1½-pound beef flank steak
1 large fresh poblano chile pepper (about 3 ounces) (see tip, page 53)
1 teaspoon cooking oil
⅓ cup chopped onion
1 clove garlic, minced
¼ cup plain fat-free yogurt
¼ cup light dairy sour cream
¼ teaspoon salt
1 tablespoon snipped fresh cilantro

1. For marinade, in a small bowl, combine lime juice, orange juice, cumin, the 2 cloves garlic, ½ teaspoon *salt*, and the chili power. Place beef steak and marinade in a

Corn-on-the-Cob Pudding

Try this calorie-trimmed corn pudding with frozen corn if fresh corn isn't in season.

PER SERVING: 136 cal., 2 g total fat (1 g sat. fat), 1 mg chol., 225 mg sodium, 22 g carb., 2 g fiber, 7 g pro. Exchanges: 1.5 starch, 0.5 very lean meat. Carb choices: 1.5.

3 ears fresh sweet corn or 1½ cups frozen whole kernel corn, thawed
Nonstick cooking spray
1 tablespoon olive oil
1 cup finely chopped onion
12 ounces Italian bread, cut into 1-inch pieces (6 cups)
2 to 3 fresh jalapeño chile peppers, seeded and finely chopped*
2 cups fat-free milk
1 cup refrigerated or frozen egg product, thawed

1. If using fresh corn, cut corn from cobs; set aside. Lightly coat a 2-quart square baking dish with cooking spray; set aside. In a large skillet, heat oil over medium heat. Add onion; cook for 3 to 4 minutes or until onion is tender, stirring occasionally. Stir in corn. Cook and stir for 2 minutes more. Remove from heat; cool slightly.

2. In a large bowl, toss together bread, corn mixture, and chile peppers. In a medium bowl, combine milk and egg; add to bread mixture. Transfer to prepared baking dish. Cover and chill for 2 to 24 hours.

3. Preheat oven to 350°F. Bake, uncovered, about 45 minutes or until lightly browned and set in center. Let stand on a wire rack for 10 minutes before serving. Makes 12 (^{2}/₃-cup) servings.

Test Kitchen Tip: Because chile peppers contain volatile oils that can burn your skin and eyes, avoid direct contact with them as much as possible. When working with chile peppers, wear plastic or rubber gloves. If your bare hands do touch the peppers, wash your hands and nails well with soap and water.

Corn-on-the-Cob Pudding

from our kitchens
to yours

Stuffed Peppers
recipe, page 61

Knowing you're not alone in dealing with diabetes helps. See how six people have learned to mix diabetes-friendly cooking with their strong sense of family and dedication to cultural and holiday traditions. Their successes are worth celebrating!

catering to diabetes

Pat LeGrand puts a lot of love into her cooking—and her Cleveland business that caters to people with diabetes. Her family and their favorite dishes are the inspiration. "We can eat our traditional foods as long as they're adjusted a little," she says.

When her mother was diagnosed with type 2 diabetes five years ago, Pat had no idea her life would take a dramatically different direction as a result. Pat was a high-powered corporate auditor in Cleveland who just wanted to help her 80-year-old mother, Iris, eat better to control her diabetes. Now she owns the first restaurant in the United States that caters mainly to people with diabetes.

"When Mother was diagnosed, I didn't know how much diabetes could be affected by diet and lifestyle," says Pat. "Food is normal and natural. It's a source of solace. When you find out you have diabetes, you're told all the things you've come to love and enjoy are not good for you."

Iris found it hard to cook differently and start exercising. She vacillated between not eating and having low blood glucose, then eating too much and having high blood glucose. And it upset Pat to see her mother, a great cook, eating food she didn't like.

Pat knew she had to help, but her work schedule limited her. Pat tackled her mother's diabetes just as she would solve a problem at work. She started by conducting research about diabetes from health organizations. Pat then began cooking for her mother. "I realized that there was nothing I couldn't cook for someone with diabetes," Pat says.

Pat had been cooking for her mother for about a year when opportunity knocked. Her company downsized and Pat was laid off. She realized she wanted to start her own business, but she didn't know what it would be. While cooking for her mother one day, Pat thought, "I wish someone would open a restaurant so I wouldn't have to keep cooking the way I do." But there was no such place. She realized her wish was the "it" idea she'd been looking for for her business. Within two years A Touch of Sugar, Pat's restaurant in Cleveland, was born.

When someone had diabetes, my Southern family called it having 'a touch of sugar,' which inspired the name of my restaurant.

—Pat LeGrand, Cleveland

**Oven-Fried Chicken Breasts,
Macaroni and Cheese**
recipes, page 58

Pictured (far left) outside her Cleveland
restaurant with her daughters and mom,
from left: Rijalon, Iris, Pat, and Eden.

Vegetable Chili and
Buttermilk Corn Muffins
recipes, pages 62 and 58

Sweet Potato Pie
recipe, page 62

Oven-Fried Chicken Breasts

Chicken crisps in the oven rather than in a deep-fat fryer and the result is perfect picnic fare. Pictured on page 57.

PER SERVING: 267 cal., 2 g total fat (1 g sat. fat), 88 mg chol., 336 mg sodium, 23 g carb., 1 g fiber, 37 g pro. Exchanges: 1.5 starch, 4.5 very lean meat. Carb choices: 1.5.

6 skinless, boneless chicken breast halves (about 2 pounds total)
1 cup buttermilk
  Olive oil nonstick cooking spray
1¼ cups crushed cornflakes
1 teaspoon garlic powder or dried minced garlic
1 teaspoon onion powder or dried minced onion
1 teaspoon paprika
½ teaspoon ground black pepper

1. In a large resealable plastic bag, combine chicken and buttermilk. Seal the bag; turn bag to coat chicken. Marinate chicken in the refrigerator for 2 to 8 hours, turning the bag occasionally.

2. Preheat oven to 400°F. Line a baking sheet with foil; coat foil with nonstick cooking spray. Drain chicken, discarding buttermilk.

3. In another large resealable plastic bag, combine crushed cornflakes, garlic powder, onion powder, paprika, and pepper; seal bag. Shake well to combine. Add chicken, one piece at a time, and shake bag to coat chicken well.

4. Place chicken on the prepared baking sheet. Coat chicken with nonstick cooking spray. Bake, uncovered, for 20 to 25 minutes or until chicken is no longer pink (170°F). Makes 6 servings.

Macaroni and Cheese

This updated version of the classic capitalizes on lower-fat ingredients. Pictured on page 57.

PER SERVING: 169 cal., 3 g total fat (2 g sat. fat), 9 mg chol., 210 mg sodium, 24 g carb., 1 g fiber, 11 g pro. Exchanges: 1.5 starch, 1 lean meat. Carb choices: 1.5.

8 ounces dried elbow macaroni
  Nonstick cooking spray
1 12-ounce can evaporated fat-free milk
½ cup refrigerated or frozen egg product, thawed, or 2 eggs, lightly beaten
2 teaspoons onion powder
½ teaspoon ground black pepper
¾ cup finely shredded Parmesan cheese (3 ounces)
¼ cup shredded reduced-fat cheddar cheese (1 ounce)
½ teaspoon paprika

1. Preheat oven to 350°F. Cook macaroni according to package directions. Drain and keep warm. Lightly coat a 2-quart baking dish with cooking spray; set aside.

2. In a medium bowl, whisk evaporated milk, eggs, onion powder, and pepper. Add drained macaroni, Parmesan cheese, and cheddar cheese; mix well.

3. Spread macaroni mixture in prepared baking dish. Sprinkle with paprika. Bake about 25 minutes or until heated through. Makes 9 (about ½-cup) servings.

Buttermilk Corn Muffins

These muffins are typical of Southern corn bread, which is less sweet than the Northern version. Pictured on page 57.

PER MUFFIN: 92 cal., 2 g total fat (0 g sat. fat), 1 mg chol., 129 mg sodium, 15 g carb., 1 g fiber, 3 g pro. Exchanges: 1 starch. Carb choices: 1.

1 cup all-purpose flour
¾ cup yellow cornmeal
1 tablespoon sugar or sugar substitute* equivalent to 1 tablespoon sugar (optional)
2 teaspoons baking powder
1 cup buttermilk
¼ cup refrigerated or frozen egg product, thawed, or 1 egg, lightly beaten
1 tablespoon canola oil
1 tablespoon lower-fat stick margarine, melted
1 teaspoon vanilla
½ teaspoon butter flavoring

1. Preheat oven to 400°F. Lightly coat twelve 2½-inch muffin cups with *nonstick cooking spray*. In a large bowl, stir together flour, cornmeal, sugar (if desired), baking powder, and ¼ teaspoon *salt*.

2. In a small bowl, whisk together buttermilk, egg, oil, margarine, vanilla, and butter flavoring. Add buttermilk mixture all at once to flour mixture; stir just until moistened. Don't overmix; batter should be slightly lumpy.

3. Spoon batter into prepared muffin cups. Bake about 15 minutes or until a toothpick inserted in centers comes out clean. Cool in muffin cups on a wire rack for 5 minutes. Remove from muffin cups. Serve warm. Makes 12.

Sugar Substitutes: Choose from Splenda granular or Sweet'N Low bulk or packets. Follow package directions to use product amount equivalent to 1 tablespoon sugar.

Chicken, Brown Rice, and Vegetable Skillet

If you need to limit gluten in your diet, this hearty gluten-free entrée is a tasty solution, and you won't know the difference.

PER SERVING: 290 cal., 5 g total fat (1 g sat. fat), 48 mg chol., 661 mg sodium, 39 g carb., 6 g fiber, 23 g pro. Exchanges: 1 vegetable, 2 starch, 2 very lean meat, 0.5 fat. Carb choices: 2.5.

- 2 tablespoons dried porcini mushrooms
- 2 teaspoons olive oil
- 1/2 cup chopped onion
- 1/2 cup sliced celery
- 1/2 cup bite-size strips red or green sweet pepper
- 1 14-ounce can reduced-sodium chicken broth
- 1 1/2 cups instant brown rice
- 4 medium carrots, cut into thin bite-size strips
- 2 cups chopped cooked skinless chicken breast (10 ounces)
- 1 13.75- or 14-ounce can artichoke hearts, drained and halved
- 1 teaspoon poultry seasoning
- 1/2 teaspoon garlic-herb salt-free seasoning blend
- 1/4 teaspoon salt
- 1/4 teaspoon garlic powder
- 1/4 teaspoon ground black pepper

1. Place mushrooms in a small bowl; add enough boiling *water* to cover. Let stand for 5 minutes; drain. Snip mushrooms and set aside.

2. In a very large skillet, heat oil over medium heat. Add onion, celery, and sweet pepper; cook about 4 minutes or until vegetables are tender, stirring mixture occasionally.

3. Add chicken broth and mushrooms to skillet. Bring to boiling. Stir in uncooked rice. Return to boiling; reduce heat. Cover and simmer for 5 minutes. Stir in carrots. Cover and cook for 5 minutes more. Stir in chicken, artichokes, poultry seasoning, seasoning blend, salt, garlic powder, and pepper. Heat through. Makes 5 (1 1/3-cup) servings.

Chicken, Brown Rice, and Vegetable Skillet

(10 menu picks)

Pat LeGrand is constantly trying new foods, but here are a few secrets to her top-selling items.

1. **Oven-Fried Chicken Breasts:** Pat dips the pieces into low-fat buttermilk, then bakes them instead of frying.
2. **Macaroni and Cheese:** Dreamfields pasta is Pat's secret—it has more fiber than regular pasta.
3. **Meat Loaf:** Pat chooses a lean ground meat for her meat loaf and uses whole wheat bread crumbs.
4. **Turkey Burgers:** Use lean ground turkey breast.
5. **Sweet Potato Fries:** Sweet potatoes have more vitamins than regular potatoes. They're baked rather than fried.
6. **Vegetable Lasagna:** No-salt-added tomato products, low-fat cheeses, and vegetables make this healthful.
7. **Stuffed Peppers:** Pat stuffs the peppers with lean ground turkey and high-fiber brown rice.
8. **Chicken, Brown Rice, and Vegetable Skillet:** This is a gluten-free item for people who have celiac disease.
9. **Turkey and Dressing:** Originally on the menu only for Thanksgiving and Christmas, roast turkey and the trimmings are popular with Pat's guests year-round.
10. **Sweet Potato Pie:** This is the best-selling dessert. Low-fat dairy products keep it light.

Vegetable Lasagna

Vegetable Lasagna

No-boil noodles make this tempting crowd-size lasagna easy; vegetables make it good for you.

PER SERVING: 287 cal., 9 g total fat (5 g sat. fat), 49 mg chol., 465 mg sodium, 35 g carb., 6 g fiber, 18 g pro. Exchanges: 2 vegetable, 1.5 starch, 1.5 lean meat, 0.5 fat. Carb choices: 2.

- 2 **10-ounce packages frozen mixed vegetables**
- **Nonstick cooking spray**
- 2 **14.5-ounce cans no-salt-added diced tomatoes, undrained**
- 1 **28-ounce can no-salt-added crushed tomatoes**
- 1 **tablespoon dried Italian seasoning, crushed**
- $1/2$ **teaspoon salt**
- $1/2$ **teaspoon garlic powder**
- 12 **no-boil lasagna noodles**
- 1 **15-ounce carton part-skim ricotta cheese**
- 1 **10-ounce package frozen chopped spinach, thawed and well drained**
- 2 **cups shredded part-skim mozzarella cheese**
- $1/4$ **cup grated Parmesan cheese**

1. Preheat oven to 375°F. Cook vegetables according to package directions; drain and set aside. Lightly coat a 3-quart rectangular baking dish with cooking spray.

2. In a large bowl, stir together diced tomatoes, undrained crushed tomatoes, Italian seasoning, salt, and garlic powder.

3. Spread 1 cup of the tomato mixture in the prepared dish. Arrange 4 lasagna noodles crosswise on top of the tomato mixture, overlapping the noodles slightly. Spoon $2/3$ cup of the ricotta cheese in small spoonfuls onto the noodles; spread carefully over noodles. Top with a third of the drained spinach and a third of the vegetables. Sprinkle evenly with $1/2$ cup of the mozzarella cheese.

4. Repeat layering with half of remaining tomato mixture, 4 noodles, $2/3$ cup of remaining ricotta cheese, half of remaining spinach, half of remaining vegetables, and $1/2$ cup of remaining mozzarella cheese.

5. Repeat layering with the remaining 4 noodles, remaining ricotta cheese, remaining spinach, remaining vegetables, and $1/2$ cup of remaining mozzarella cheese. Spoon remaining tomato mixture on top.

6. Cover dish with foil; place on a foil-lined baking sheet. Bake for 40 minutes. Sprinkle with the remaining $1/2$ cup mozzarella cheese and the Parmesan cheese.

7. Bake, uncovered, for 10 to 15 minutes more or until noodles are tender and lasagna is heated through. Let stand for 15 minutes before serving. Makes 10 servings.

Stuffed Peppers

Peppers serve as edible bowls for the turkey filling. It is fancy enough for a party. Pictured on page 54.

PER SERVING: 220 cal., 8 g total fat (2 g sat. fat), 60 mg chol., 337 mg sodium, 21 g carb., 4 g fiber, 16 g pro. Exchanges: 1.5 vegetable, 1 starch, 1.5 lean meat, 0.5 fat. Carb choices: 1.5.

- 3 **large yellow, green, and/or red sweet peppers (8 to 10 ounces each)**
- 1 **pound uncooked ground turkey or extra-lean ground beef**
- $1/4$ **cup chopped onion**
- $1^1/2$ **cups cooked brown rice**
- $1/2$ **cup frozen stir-fry vegetables (yellow, green, and red peppers and onion) or other frozen mixed vegetables, thawed**
- $1/2$ **cup purchased mild salsa**
- $1^1/2$ **teaspoons garlic-herb salt-free seasoning blend**
- 1 **teaspoon poultry seasoning**
- $1/4$ **teaspoon salt**
- $1/3$ **cup soft whole wheat bread crumbs**
- 1 **tablespoon 40 to 50 percent vegetable oil spread, melted**
- $1/2$ **teaspoon paprika**

1. Preheat oven to 350°F. Halve peppers lengthwise; remove seeds and membranes. In a Dutch oven, cook peppers in enough boiling water to cover for 2 minutes. Drain; place peppers, cut sides up, in a 13×9×2-inch baking pan. Set aside.

2. For filling, in a large skillet, cook turkey and onion until turkey is no longer pink, breaking up turkey during cooking. If necessary, drain off fat. Stir in cooked rice, vegetables, salsa, seasoning blend, poultry seasoning, and salt. Spoon filling into pepper halves. Pour $1/2$ cup water around the stuffed peppers.

3. For topping, in a small bowl, combine crumbs, melted spread, and paprika. Sprinkle onto stuffed peppers. Cover; bake for 30 minutes. Bake, uncovered, for 5 minutes more. Makes 6 servings.

Vegetable Chili

Salt-free tomato products and seasoning blend keep the sodium down. Serve it after caroling or sledding. Pictured on page 57.

PER SERVING: 209 cal., 2 g total fat (0 g sat. fat), 0 mg chol., 375 mg sodium, 42 g carb., 11 g fiber, 10 g pro. Exchanges: 2 vegetable, 2 starch. Carb choices: 3.

  Nonstick cooking spray
1 teaspoon canola oil
1 cup chopped onion
1 cup chopped green sweet pepper
2 cloves garlic, minced, or
  1 teaspoon bottled minced garlic
1 14.5-ounce can no-salt-added diced tomatoes or stewed tomatoes, undrained
1 8-ounce can no-salt-added tomato sauce
1 cup water
4¹/₂ teaspoons chili powder
1 teaspoon garlic-herb salt-free seasoning blend
1 teaspoon ground cumin
¹/₈ teaspoon salt
1 15- to 16-ounce can kidney beans, rinsed and drained
1 cup frozen mixed vegetables
¹/₄ cup light dairy sour cream (optional)
  Coarsely snipped fresh cilantro (optional)
¹/₈ teaspoon chili powder (optional)

1. Lightly coat an unheated large saucepan or Dutch oven with nonstick cooking spray. Preheat over medium-high heat. Add oil; swirl to coat the bottom of the pan. Add onion, sweet pepper, and garlic to hot oil; cook for 8 to 10 minutes or until pepper is tender, stirring often. If necessary, reduce heat to prevent burning.

2. Add tomatoes, tomato sauce, the water, the 4¹/₂ teaspoons chili powder, seasoning blend, cumin, and salt. Bring to boiling; reduce heat. Cover; simmer for 15 minutes.

3. Stir in kidney beans and mixed vegetables. Return to boiling; reduce heat. Simmer, uncovered, about 10 minutes more or until vegetables are tender.

4. If desired, top each serving with sour cream; sprinkle with cilantro and the ¹/₈ teaspoon chili powder. Makes 4 (1¹/₂-cup) servings.

Sweet Potato Pie

Lemon accents the flavor of this holiday-perfect pumpkinlike pie. Pictured on page 57.

PER SERVING: 218 cal., 5 g total fat (1 g sat. fat), 1 mg chol., 119 mg sodium, 38 g carb., 3 g fiber, 5 g pro. Exchanges: 2.5 carb., 1 fat. Carb choices: 2.5.

1 recipe Oil Pastry (see recipe, below)
2¹/₄ pounds sweet potatoes, peeled, cooked, and mashed*
1 cup evaporated fat-free milk
¹/₂ cup sugar**
¹/₂ cup refrigerated or frozen egg product, thawed, or 2 eggs, lightly beaten
2 teaspoons ground cinnamon
2 teaspoons vanilla
1 teaspoon butter flavoring
¹/₄ teaspoon ground nutmeg
¹/₄ teaspoon lemon extract
³/₄ cup frozen light whipped dessert topping, thawed (optional)
  Ground nutmeg (optional)

1. Preheat oven to 375°F. Prepare Oil Pastry. On a well-floured surface, use your hands to slightly flatten dough. Roll dough from center to edge into a 12-inch circle. To transfer pastry, wrap it around the rolling pin. Unroll pastry into a 9-inch pie plate. Ease pastry into pie plate, being careful not to stretch pastry. Trim pastry to ¹/₂ inch beyond edge of pie plate. Fold under extra pastry. Flute or crimp edge as desired. Do not prick crust.

2. For filling, in a large bowl, combine mashed sweet potatoes, evaporated milk, sugar, eggs, cinnamon, vanilla, butter flavoring, the ¹/₄ teaspoon nutmeg, and the lemon extract; whisk until nearly smooth. Pour sweet potato filling into pastry-lined pie plate.

3. To prevent overbrowning, cover edge with foil. Bake for 25 minutes. Remove foil. Bake for 25 to 30 minutes more or until a knife comes out clean.

4. Cool the pie on a wire rack. Cover and chill within 2 hours. If desired, top each serving with whipped topping; sprinkle with additional nutmeg. Makes 12 servings.

Oil Pastry: In a medium bowl, stir together 1¹/₃ cups all-purpose flour and ¹/₄ teaspoon salt. Add ¹/₄ cup canola oil and ¹/₄ cup fat-free milk all at once to flour mixture. Stir lightly with a fork until combined (dough will appear crumbly). Use your hands to gently work dough into a ball.

*Test Kitchen Tip: To cook sweet potatoes, peel sweet potatoes. Cut into 1¹/₂-inch chunks. In a covered large saucepan, cook sweet potatoes in enough boiling water

Butter-Rum Oatmeal Cookies

to cover for 20 to 25 minutes or until very tender. Drain. Beat potatoes until smooth, using an electric mixer (you should have about 3¼ cups sweet potatoes). Cool slightly.

**Test Kitchen Tip: We don't recommend sugar substitutes for this recipe.

Butter Rum Oatmeal Cookies

This soft, eggless cookie makes a delightful snack—especially with a hot cup of tea.

PER COOKIE: 67 cal., 1 g total fat (0 g sat. fat), 0 mg chol., 36 mg sodium, 12 g carb., 0 g fiber, 1 g pro. Exchanges: 1 carb. Carb choices: 1.

Butter-flavor nonstick cooking spray
½ **cup packed brown sugar***
6 **tablespoons lower-fat stick margarine**
1 **teaspoon ground cinnamon**
¼ **teaspoon baking soda**
1 **tablespoon light-color corn syrup**
1 **teaspoon vanilla**
1 **teaspoon butter flavoring**
¼ **teaspoon rum flavoring**
1 **cup all-purpose flour**
¾ **cup rolled oats**
¼ **cup raisins**

1. Preheat oven to 375°F. Coat 2 cookie sheets with cooking spray; set aside. In a bowl, combine brown sugar, margarine, cinnamon, and baking soda. Beat with an electric mixer on medium speed until combined.

2. Stir in corn syrup, vanilla, butter flavoring, and rum flavoring. Using a wooden spoon, stir flour into margarine mixture. Stir in oats and raisins. Drop dough by rounded teaspoons 2 inches apart on prepared cookie sheets.

3. Bake for 8 to 10 minutes or until light brown around edges. Transfer to wire racks; cool. Makes 24 cookies.

*Test Kitchen Tip: We don't recommend sugar substitutes for this recipe.

Christmas Ribbon Salad recipe, page 66

Terry (right) with his grandson, Peter, enjoy reading a storybook by the fire before Christmas dinner. Terry learned early on that his diabetes didn't have to change his holiday traditions—like eating Christmas Ribbon Salad.

(terry adams)

celebrating for life

Terry and Helene Adams learned early on that Terry's diabetes need not change their holiday traditions. Every Christmas Eve, their family—from their young grandson, Peter, to Helene's elderly mother, Edythe Frette—gathers at their Ames, Iowa, home for a cozy Scandinavian-style dinner. Helene still prepares their favorite Norwegian treats, but she's careful to add a few healthful dishes of her own such as baked fish, spinach salad, and brown rice pudding. Everybody eats the same food, and Terry keeps an eye on his portions. If he indulges a little that day, he knows he'll get back on track the next morning.

In his early 70s, Terry has more energy and feels better than he has in a long time. "He's found the fountain of youth," Helene says. His diagnosis of diabetes more than seven years ago provided the incentive to help him turn his health around.

The journey started at a routine physical in October 2001. Terry's doctor told him he had type 2 diabetes. His doctor's stern warning was followed by a gentle yet firm nudge from Helene. "If you don't take care of yourself, you could lose your eyesight," said his wife of more than 40 years. "I'll take care of you whatever happens, but I'd hate to see you not be able to enjoy things you love, such as reading and playing music." Terry decided to take care of his diabetes and signed on for diabetes counseling.

The real solution, Terry learned, wasn't choosing between diet and exercise—it had to be both. Initially, he had all the classic excuses for not exercising. "Walking at the gym was a challenge," he says. Then he discovered headphones, and soon marching music made the time slip away. He now walks around the neighborhood for an hour on most days.

Terry is very proud of himself, as he should be. "I feel better than I have in a long time," he says. The "fountain of youth"—in the form of eating right, exercising, and monitoring blood glucose—has definitely let Terry live the life he loves.

"Terry's diagnosis of diabetes provided the incentive to help him turn his health around."

—Helene Adams,
Ames, Iowa

Spinach Salad with Glazed Almonds
recipe, page 66

Christmas Ribbon Salad

Layer the holiday colors of green, white, and red.
Pictured on page 64.

- **2 4-serving-size packages sugar-free lime-flavor gelatin**
- **1 4-serving-size package sugar-free lemon-flavor gelatin**
- **1 8-ounce tub light cream cheese, softened**
- **1/2 cup unsweetened pineapple juice**
- **1 cup frozen light whipped dessert topping, thawed**
- **1 4-serving-size package sugar-free raspberry-flavor gelatin**
- **1 4-serving-size package sugar-free cherry-flavor gelatin**

1. In a medium bowl, combine lime-flavor gelatin and 2 1/2 cups *boiling water;* stir until gelatin is dissolved. Divide mixture among sixteen 4- to 6-ounce wineglasses or dessert dishes, spooning about 2 tablespoons into each glass. (Or pour mixture into a 3-quart rectangular baking dish.) Cover; chill for 1 to 2 hours or until firm.

2. In a large bowl, combine lemon-flavor gelatin and 1 1/2 cups *boiling water;* stir until gelatin is dissolved. Whisk in cream cheese until melted and smooth. Stir in pineapple juice. Let stand for 30 minutes. Gently fold in dessert topping. Divide gelatin mixture among wineglasses, spooning about 3 tablespoons onto green layer in each. (Or carefully pour lemon gelatin mixture over lime layer in baking dish.) Cover and chill for 1 to 2 hours or until firm.

3. In a medium bowl, combine raspberry- and cherry-flavor gelatins and 2 1/2 cups *boiling water;* stir until gelatin is dissolved. Let stand about 1 hour or until cool. Divide mixture among wineglasses, spooning about 2 tablespoons onto lemon gelatin layer in each. (Or carefully pour mixture over the lemon gelatin layer in baking dish.) Cover and chill for 2 to 3 hours or until firm. Makes 16 servings.

Spinach Salad with Glazed Almonds

Use granulated sugar for the caramel coating on the nuts, but switch to sugar substitute for the dressing, if you wish. Pictured on page 65.

- **Nonstick cooking spray**
- **1/3 cup sliced almonds**
- **2 teaspoons sugar**
- **1 10-ounce package fresh spinach**
- **1 cup sliced fresh strawberries**
- **2/3 cup sliced celery**
- **2 green onions, sliced**
- **1/4 cup olive oil**
- **1/4 cup red wine vinegar**
- **1 teaspoon sugar or sugar substitute* equivalent to 1 teaspoon sugar**
- **1/4 teaspoon salt**
- **2 drops bottled hot pepper sauce**

1. For glazed almonds, line a baking sheet with foil. Coat foil with nonstick cooking spray. In a small heavy skillet, combine almonds and the 2 teaspoons sugar. Cook over medium-high heat until sugar begins to melt, shaking skillet occasionally. Do not stir. Reduce heat to low. Continue cooking until sugar is golden brown, stirring occasionally. Remove skillet from heat. Pour nut mixture onto the prepared baking sheet. Cool completely. Break into clusters.

2. Meanwhile, in a large bowl, combine spinach, berries, celery, and green onions; set aside.

3. For dressing, in a bowl, whisk together oil, vinegar, the 1 teaspoon sugar, salt, and hot pepper sauce.

4. Drizzle dressing onto spinach mixture; toss gently to coat. To serve, top salad with glazed almonds. Makes 8 (1 1/4-cup) servings.

*Sugar Substitutes: Choose from Splenda granular, Equal Spoonful or packets, or Sweet'N Low bulk or packets. Follow package directions to use product amount equivalent to 1 teaspoon sugar.

Seasoned Cod

A simple sprinkling of paprika and seasoned salt allows
the fresh flavor of the fish to take center stage.

PER SERVING: 93 cal., 1 g total fat (0 g sat. fat), 48 mg chol., 156 mg
sodium, 0 g carb., 0 g fiber, 20 g pro. Exchanges: 3 very lean meat. Carb
choices: 0.

- **2** **pounds fresh or frozen skinless cod fillets, $3/4$ to 1 inch
  thick**
- **1** **teaspoon paprika**
- **$1/2$** **teaspoon seasoned salt**
- **Lemon wedges and/or fresh parsley sprigs (optional)**

1. Thaw fish, if frozen. Rinse fish; pat dry with paper
towels. In a small bowl, combine paprika and seasoned
salt; sprinkle onto both sides of fish. Measure the
thickness of the fish.

2. Preheat broiler. Place fish on the greased unheated
rack of a broiler pan. Broil 4 inches from the heat for
4 to 6 minutes per $1/2$-inch thickness or until fish flakes
easily when tested with a fork. If desired, garnish with
lemon wedges and/or parsley sprigs. Makes 8 servings.

Microwave Directions: Prepare as directed in Step 1. In
a 2-quart square microwave-safe baking dish, arrange
fish in a single layer (do not overlap). Cover with vented
plastic wrap. Microwave on 100 percent power (high) for
5 to 7 minutes or until fish flakes easily when tested with
a fork, turning dish once halfway through cooking, if
necessary. Serve as above.

Quick Tip

The key is to emphasize
healthy eating as a lifestyle,
not engaging in a crash
diet, Terry points out. Yes,
you must cut back, but you
can eat everything—in
moderation. Terry loves to
eat pie, for example, but
limits himself to having
just two slices of his
favorites a year.

Dilled Peas and Mushrooms

These colorful peas are the perfect companion to
Seasoned Cod (see recipe, left).

PER SERVING: 78 cal., 2 g total fat (0 g sat. fat), 0 mg chol., 154 mg sodium,
11 g carb., 4 g fiber, 4 g pro. Exchanges: 0.5 vegetable, 0.5 starch,
0.5 fat. Carb choices: 1.

- **2** **10-ounce packages frozen peas with pearl onions**
- **1** **small red sweet pepper, seeded and coarsely
  chopped ($2/3$ cup)**
- **2** **cups sliced fresh mushrooms**
- **1** **tablespoon olive oil**
- **1** **tablespoon snipped fresh dill or 1 teaspoon dried dill**
- **$1/4$** **teaspoon salt**
- **Dash ground black pepper**

1. In a covered large saucepan, cook peas and onions
and sweet pepper in a small amount of boiling water
about 5 minutes or until crisp-tender; drain well. Transfer
to a medium bowl; set aside.

2. In the same saucepan, cook mushrooms in hot oil
about 5 minutes or until tender, stirring occasionally.
Stir in dill, salt, and pepper. Return mixture to saucepan;
heat through. Makes 8 ($1/2$-cup) servings.

(priscilla fernandez)
now we're cooking

Every time Priscilla (Pinky) Fernandez attended her diabetes class, she felt guilty. "Here we were, getting all these great new recipes and I wasn't changing a thing. I wasn't even opening my book," she admits. Week after week, Pinky looked around at her classmates, all newly diagnosed or trying to bring diabetes under control. She began to realize that they, like her, were struggling with the changes they needed to make. "I knew I should change the way I was eating. My husband and I were going out to dinner all the time, so I was being tempted by all the wrong things," Pinky says. "What's really sad is that I love to cook! I wondered why they weren't showing our class how to plan a perfect diabetic meal. I wanted some hands-on practice, so I decided to offer my home and see if anyone else wanted to cook together."

The next week at the last class, Pinky announced: "We have all these great recipes and need to learn to cook a whole new way. Who would like to form a diabetic cooking club to meet at my house?" Although only one person raised her hand, a group eventually was formed. They called themselves DDD for Diabetic Dining by Design.

When the group members first gathered at Pinky's house to lay the ground rules, they realized they had a unique opportunity not only to eat more healthfully but to learn about foods from different cultures and to try unfamiliar ingredients. Each person takes a turn at picking out a menu, shopping, and preparing food ahead of time. Members can make recipes from nondiabetic cookbooks but must modify recipes to diabetic standards. Everyone except the cook helps with cleaning up.

Pinky keeps a binder of the group's menus so members can copy recipes they'd like to make at home. Unlike her diabetes class binder that stayed shut from week to week, the group binder is a frequent reference. "This group is like family to me now," Pinky says. "And our binder is the family cookbook."

> " Wanting hands-on practice, I offered my home to see if anyone else wanted to form a cooking club. "
>
> —Pinky Fernandez

Colorados (Red Bean Soup)
recipe, page 71

Cuban-Style Swordfish
recipe, page 70

Priscilla (Pinky) Fernandez (above right) cooks with other club members in her home. Although she is Mexican American, her cooking style reflects her husband's Cuban roots—fish, beans, and herbs.

Grilled Vegetable-Lamb Skewers
recipe, page 71

Chicken-Tofu Stir-Fry

Chicken-Tofu Stir-Fry

Mix and match the vegetable options to create
a new dish every time you make this stir-fry.

PER SERVING: 285 cal., 9 g total fat (1 g sat. fat), 32 mg chol., 331 mg
sodium, 30 g carb., 4 g fiber, 20 g pro. Exchanges: 1 vegetable,
1.5 starch, 2 lean meat, 0.5 fat. Carb choices: 2.

  2   tablespoons olive oil
  2   tablespoons orange juice
  1   tablespoon reduced-sodium soy sauce
  1   tablespoon Worcestershire sauce
  1   tablespoon grated fresh ginger
  1   teaspoon dry mustard
  1   teaspoon ground turmeric
  8   ounces cooked chicken breast, cubed
  8   ounces tub-style extra-firm tofu (fresh bean curd),
      drained and cubed
  2   medium carrots or 2 stalks celery, bias-sliced
  1   cup pea pods and/or sliced fresh mushrooms
  3   green onions, cut into $1/2$-inch-long pieces
  1   medium red and/or green sweet pepper, cut into thin
      bite-size strips
  2   cups chopped baby bok choy and/or fresh
      bean sprouts
  3   cups hot cooked brown or white rice

1. In a large bowl, stir together 1 tablespoon of the oil,
the orange juice, soy sauce, Worcestershire sauce, ginger,
mustard, and turmeric. Add chicken and tofu; stir to
coat. Cover and chill for up to 4 hours.

2. In a very large nonstick skillet, heat remaining
1 tablespoon oil over medium-high heat. Add carrot or
celery; cook and stir for 2 minutes. Add pea pods and/or
mushrooms; cook and stir for 2 minutes. Add green

onions and sweet pepper; cook and stir for 2 minutes.
Stir in bok choy and/or bean sprouts.

3. Add undrained chicken mixture; heat through.
Serve with hot cooked rice. Makes 6 (1-cup stir-fry plus
$1/2$ cup rice) servings.

Cuban-Style Swordfish

With grilling and broiling options, this fish-and-salsa
medley makes a great meal any time of year.
Pictured on page 69.

PER SERVING: 190 cal., 8 g total fat (2 g sat. fat), 43 mg chol.,
254 mg sodium, 6 g carb., 3 g fiber, 24 g pro. Exchanges: 1 vegetable,
3 very lean meat, 1.5 fat. Carb choices: 0.5.

  1   pound fresh or frozen swordfish steaks,
      cut 1 inch thick
  1   large clove garlic, halved
  2   tablespoons lime juice
$1/2$ teaspoon ground cumin
$1/4$ teaspoon ground black pepper
$1/8$ teaspoon salt
     Nonstick cooking spray
  1   recipe Fresh Tomato Salsa (see recipe, below)

1. Thaw fish, if frozen. Rinse fish; pat dry with paper
towels. Cut fish into 4 serving-size pieces. Rub fish on
both sides with garlic. Place fish in a shallow glass dish;
drizzle with lime juice. Cover; marinate in the refrigerator
for 30 minutes, turning once. Drain fish. In a bowl, combine
cumin, black pepper, and salt; sprinkle onto fish.

2. Coat a cold grill rack with cooking spray. Grill fish
on rack of an uncovered grill directly over medium heat
for 8 to 12 minutes or until fish flakes easily when tested
with a fork, turning once halfway through grilling. Serve
swordfish with Fresh Tomato Salsa. Makes 4 servings.

Fresh Tomato Salsa: In a medium bowl, combine 1 cup
chopped red and/or yellow tomato; $1/4$ cup chopped
tomatillo; $1/4$ cup chopped avocado; 2 tablespoons snipped
fresh cilantro; 1 medium fresh jalapeño pepper, seeded
and finely chopped (see tip, page 53); 1 minced clove
garlic; 1 tablespoon lime juice; $1/8$ teaspoon salt; and
$1/8$ teaspoon ground black pepper. Serve immediately
or cover and chill for up to 4 hours.

Broiling Directions: Preheat broiler. Coat unheated rack
of a broiler pan with cooking spray. Broil fish on unheated
rack of broiler pan about 4 inches from heat for 8 to
12 minutes or until fish flakes easily when tested with a
fork, turning fish once halfway through broiling.

Grilled Vegetable-Lamb Skewers

You can make your own garam masala, but you can buy the spice blend as well. Pictured on page 69.

PER SERVING: 232 cal., 4 g total fat (1 g sat. fat), 71 mg chol., 226 mg sodium, 22 g carb., 5 g fiber, 27 g pro. Exchanges: 1 starch, 1 vegetable, 3 very lean meat, 0.5 fat. Carb choices: 1.5.

- 1 **pound lean boneless lamb**
- $1/4$ **cup snipped fresh cilantro**
- 2 **tablespoons chopped onion**
- 2 **tablespoons lime juice or lemon juice**
- 4 **cloves garlic, minced**
- 2 **teaspoons grated fresh ginger**
- 1 **medium jalapeño pepper, seeded and finely chopped (optional) (see tip, page 53)**
- 1 **teaspoon Homemade Garam Masala (see recipe, below) or purchased garam masala**
- $1/4$ **teaspoon salt**
- 2 **cups assorted vegetables (such as $1^1/2$-inch chunks of yellow summer squash or eggplant, red onion wedges, or baby pattypan squash)**
  Nonstick cooking spray
- $1^1/2$ **cups water**
- $3/4$ **cup bulgur**
- 2 **tablespoons snipped fresh cilantro**

1. Trim fat from lamb; cut into $1^1/2$-inch pieces. Place lamb in a resealable plastic bag set in a shallow dish; set aside.

2. In a small bowl, combine $1/4$ cup cilantro, onion, lime juice, garlic, ginger, jalapeño pepper (if using), garam masala, and salt. Add to lamb; seal bag. Turn to coat. Chill for 4 to 6 hours.

3. On four 12-inch-long metal skewers, alternately thread lamb and vegetable pieces, leaving a $1/4$-inch space between pieces. Discard cilantro mixture.

4. Coat a cold grill rack with cooking spray. Grill skewers on rack of uncovered grill directly over medium heat for 12 to 14 minutes or until lamb is just pink in center, turning once.

5. In a saucepan, combine water and bulgur. Bring to boiling; reduce heat. Cover and simmer about 15 minutes or until tender. Drain bulgur; stir in 2 tablespoons cilantro.

6. Serve skewers with bulgur. Makes 4 (1-skewer plus $1/2$-cup bulgur) servings.

Homemade Garam Masala: In a skillet, cook 1 tablespoon cumin seeds, 1 tablespoon cardamom seeds, 1 tablespoon whole black peppercorns, 12 whole cloves, and 3 inches stick cinnamon over medium heat about 3 minutes or until aromatic. Cool. In a sealed plastic bag, crush cinnamon with a rolling pin. In a spice grinder or blender, combine the spices. Cover and grind spice mixture to a powder. Store in a covered container for up to 6 months. Makes about $1/4$ cup.

Colorados (Red Bean Soup)

To save time, soak the dry beans the day before to make this high-fiber soup. Pictured on page 68.

PER SERVING: 273 cal., 4 g total fat (1 g sat. fat), 35 mg chol., 457 mg sodium, 33 g carb., 12 g fiber, 24 g pro. Exchanges: 0.5 vegetable, 1.5 starch, 0.5 other carb., 2.5 very lean meat, 0.5 fat. Carb choices: 2.

- 1 **pound dry red kidney beans**
- $3/4$ **cup dry white wine or lower-sodium beef broth**
- 1 **medium green or red sweet pepper, chopped**
- 1 **medium onion, chopped**
- 1 **medium tomato, chopped**
- 4 **cloves garlic, minced**
- 1 **medium fresh yellow wax pepper or banana pepper, seeded and chopped**
- 1 **pound fresh beef brisket**
- 1 **ham hock**
- 1 **large russet potato**
- 1 **teaspoon salt**
- $1/2$ **teaspoon ground black pepper**

1. In a Dutch oven, combine beans and 6 cups water. Bring to boiling; reduce heat. Simmer for 2 minutes. Remove from heat. Cover; let stand for 1 hour. (Or place beans in 6 cups water. Cover; let soak in a cool place for 6 to 8 hours or overnight.) Drain and rinse beans.

2. Return beans to Dutch oven. Add 8 cups *water*, the wine, sweet pepper, onion, tomato, garlic, and wax pepper. Bring to boiling.

3. Trim brisket; cut into $3/4$-inch pieces. Add beef and ham hock to bean mixture. Return to boiling; reduce heat. Cover; simmer about $1^1/2$ hours or until beans and meat are tender. Remove hock; let cool. Mash beans slightly.

4. Peel and dice potato; stir into beans. Bring to boiling; reduce heat. Cover and simmer about 15 minutes or until potato is tender.

5. When ham is cool enough to handle, cut meat from bone; discard bone. Cut ham into bite-size pieces; stir into bean mixture. Stir in salt and black pepper. Makes 10 ($1^1/2$-cup) servings.

(nechama cohen)
building on faith

Nechama Cohen was 35 when she was diagnosed with type 1 diabetes, more than 20 years ago. At the time, Nechama was a busy mother of five children, including a set of twins. "When the doctor told me I had diabetes," Nechama says, "I wondered how I was going to go home to five children and still lead a normal life." Especially when normal meant adhering to Jewish dietary laws and an observant Jewish lifestyle.

At first, no one could answer Nechama's questions. "I didn't feel good most of the time," says Nechama. "But when I asked for help, the doctors only knew the standard treatment. I couldn't believe diabetes had to be that way." Then she and her husband, Yossie, discovered the Joslin Diabetes Center in Boston, where they took classes on diabetes.

The more Nechama learned about diabetes, the more she wanted to know. She decided to go back to school and enroll in nutrition and nursing classes. In studying nutrition, Nechama hoped to learn how to eat healthfully and still follow Jewish dietary guidelines. She went to support groups, but no one was talking about the Jewish lifestyle. Eventually, she created a network of other Jewish women with diabetes and began having monthly meetings to discuss the challenges they faced. The meetings became so large, they had to move to larger locations. Nechama approached the American Diabetes Association (ADA) to gain support for the group. In 2000, the Jewish Diabetes Association was born, with Nechama as chief executive officer.

One area the group tackled was how to adapt traditional kosher eating to adhere to diabetic eating guidelines. She began lightening her family's traditional recipes and shared the recipes in magazines. The ADA suggested she write a cookbook for Jewish people with diabetes, which resulted in *Enlitened Kosher Cooking*. "We can't put our heads in the sand," Nechama says. "Diabetes is a gift I was given. You must find joy in what you're given. Being Jewish has helped me. When you have faith, you have a tremendous strength to fall back on. I've built on that in my life."

" When I found out I had diabetes, I wondered how I was going to adhere to Jewish dietary laws and be observant of the Jewish traditions. "

—Nechama Cohen, Brooklyn, New York

It was important to Nechama to learn how to incorporate her Jewish beliefs and traditions into her diabetes meal plans. Learning how to cook for herself and her family (left and above) became very important.

Balsamic Chicken, Mock Noodle Kugel
recipes, pages 76 and 77

Orange and Fennel Salad with Citrus Vinaigrette

Using less oil keeps the dressing light.

PER SERVING: 93 cal., 5 g total fat (1 g sat. fat), 0 mg chol., 76 mg sodium, 12 g carb., 3 g fiber, 2 g pro. Exchanges: 1. 5 vegetable, 0.5 fruit, 1 fat. Carb choices: 1.

PER SERVING WITH SUBSTITUTE: same as above, except 91 cal., 11 g carb.

- 1 medium fennel bulb
- 4 cups torn romaine lettuce
- 2 cups torn radicchio ($^1/_2$ of a small head)
- 1$^1/_2$ teaspoons finely shredded orange peel (set aside)
- 2 medium oranges, peeled and sectioned
- 1 small red onion, halved and thinly sliced
- 1 recipe Citrus Vinaigrette (see recipe, right)

1. Snip enough of the fennel leaves to make 1 teaspoon; reserve for vinaigrette. If desired, reserve additional leaves for garnish. Cut off and discard fennel stalks. Remove wilted outer layers of bulb; cut off a thin slice. Cut bulb lengthwise into quarters. Thinly slice quarters; set aside.

2. On a serving platter, arrange romaine, radicchio, orange, onion, and fennel slices. If desired, top with fennel leaves. Serve salad with Citrus Vinaigrette. Makes 6 (1$^1/_2$-cup) servings.

Citrus Vinaigrette: In a small bowl, combine reserved snipped fennel leaves, 3 tablespoons white wine vinegar, 2 tablespoons olive oil, 2 tablespoons water, 2 cloves minced garlic, 1$^1/_2$ teaspoons finely shredded orange peel, 1 teaspoon sugar or sugar substitute* equivalent to 1 teaspoon sugar, $^1/_8$ teaspoon salt, and $^1/_8$ teaspoon ground black pepper; whisk until mixed. For a creamier dressing, whisk in 1 tablespoon light mayonnaise or salad dressing.

*Sugar Substitutes: Choose from Splenda granular, Equal Spoonful or packets, or Sweet'N Low bulk or packets. Follow the package directions to use product amount equivalent to 1 teaspoon sugar.

Orange and Fennel Salad with Citrus Vinaigrette

Perfect Water and Whole Wheat Challah

Serve this diabetes-friendly braided Jewish bread with dinner or for sandwiches or breakfast toast.

PER SLICE: 117 cal., 2 g total fat (0 g sat. fat), 13 mg chol., 151 mg sodium, 21 g carb., 2 g fiber, 4 g pro. Exchanges: 1.5 starch. Carb choices: 1.5.
PER SLICE WITH SUBSTITUTE: same as above, except 114 cal., 20 g carb. Carb choices: 1.

4^1/$_2$ to 5 cups all-purpose flour
2^1/$_2$ cups warm water
    (110°F to 115°F)
  1 package active dry yeast
  2 tablespoons sugar or sugar substitute* equivalent to
     2 tablespoons sugar
  2 teaspoons salt
  3 tablespoons canola oil
  1 egg
  1 egg white
2^1/$_2$ cups whole wheat flour
    Nonstick cooking spray
  1 egg yolk
  1 tablespoon water
  1 to 2 tablespoons poppy seeds, black and/or white
     sesame seeds, or rolled oats

1. In a small bowl, combine ^{1}/$_4$ cup of the all-purpose flour, ^{1}/$_4$ cup of the warm water, the yeast, and half of the sugar. Let stand at room temperature for 10 to 15 minutes or until mixture begins to bubble.

2. Meanwhile, in a large mixing bowl, stir together 2 cups of the all-purpose flour, remaining sugar, and salt. Add remaining 2^1/$_4$ cups warm water, yeast mixture, oil, egg, and egg white. Beat with an electric mixer on low to medium speed for 30 seconds, scraping sides. Beat on high speed for 3 minutes. Using a wooden spoon, stir in whole wheat flour and as much of the remaining all-purpose flour as you can.

3. Turn out dough onto a lightly floured surface. Knead in enough of the remaining all-purpose flour to make a moderately stiff dough that is smooth and elastic (6 to 8 minutes total). Cover; let rest for 10 minutes. Knead for 2 minutes more. Cover; let rest again for 10 minutes. Knead for 2 minutes. Coat a large bowl with cooking spray; add dough. Spray dough with spray. Cover; let rise in a warm place until double in size (about 1 hour).

4. Punch dough down; cover and let rise for 45 minutes. Punch dough down; divide in half. Cover and let rest for

Perfect Water and Whole Wheat Challah

10 minutes. Divide each portion of dough into three ropes (if making loaves) or 16 pieces (if making rolls).

5. For loaves, on a lightly floured surface, roll each dough portion into a 14-inch-long rope. Place ropes on a large baking sheet coated with spray. Using three ropes for each loaf, braid ropes into two loaves. Place 5 inches apart on the baking sheet. For rolls, coat two 13×9×2-inch baking pans with nonstick cooking spray; shape portions into rolls. Place 16 rolls in each pan.

6. Cover loaves or rolls; let rise in a warm place until nearly double in size (30 to 45 minutes). Preheat oven to 425°F.

7. In a bowl, combine egg yolk and the 1 tablespoon water; brush onto dough. Top with seeds or oats.

8. For loaves, bake for 10 minutes. Reduce oven temperature to 375°F. Bake for 15 to 20 minutes or until bread sounds hollow when tapped. (For rolls, bake at 425°F about 15 minutes or until tops sound hollow. Do not reduce oven temperature.)

9. Remove loaves or rolls from baking sheet or pans. Cool on wire racks. Makes 2 loaves (16 slices each) or 32 rolls.

*Sugar Substitutes: Choose from Splenda granular or Sweet'N Low bulk or packets. Follow the package directions to use product amount equivalent to 2 tablespoons sugar.

Creamy Pumpkin Soup

Instead of flour, pumpkin thickens this soup.

PER SERVING: 69 cal., 3 g total fat (0 g sat. fat), 0 mg chol., 304 mg sodium, 9 g carb., 1 g fiber, 3 g pro. Exchanges: 0.5 starch, 0.5 fat. Carb choices: 0.5.

PER SERVING WITH SUBSTITUTE: same as above, except 66 cal.

Nonstick cooking spray
- 1 tablespoon olive oil
- $3/4$ cup chopped leeks
- 2 cloves garlic, minced
- 3 cups peeled and cubed pumpkin or acorn squash
- 3 cups reduced-sodium chicken broth or homemade low-sodium chicken stock
- $1/8$ to $1/4$ teaspoon ground black pepper
- $1/8$ teaspoon ground cloves or ground nutmeg (optional)
- 1 cup light plain soymilk
- $1/2$ to 1 cup water
- 1 to 2 teaspoons sugar or sugar substitute* equivalent to 1 to 2 teaspoons sugar
- 3 tablespoons pumpkin seeds or pine nuts, toasted (optional) (see tip, page 7)

1. Lightly coat an unheated large saucepan with cooking spray. Add oil; heat over medium-high heat. Add leeks and garlic; cook and stir until leeks start to brown. Stir in pumpkin, broth, pepper, and, if desired, cloves.

2. Bring pumpkin mixture to boiling; reduce heat. Cover and simmer for 30 to 45 minutes or until pumpkin is tender. Remove from heat; cool slightly.

3. Transfer half of the pumpkin mixture to a blender or food processor; cover and blend or process until smooth. Set aside. Repeat with the remaining pumpkin mixture. Return all of the pureed mixture to the saucepan. (Or puree all of the pumpkin at once by holding an immersion blender directly in the saucepan.)

4. Stir in soymilk and enough water to reach desired consistency; heat through but do not boil. Stir in sugar to taste. Serve warm.

5. If desired, garnish with toasted pumpkin seeds or pine nuts. Makes 6 (about $3/4$-cup) servings.

*Sugar Substitutes: Choose from Splenda granular, Equal Spoonful or packets, or Sweet'N Low bulk or packets. Follow package directions to use product amount equivalent to 1 to 2 teaspoons sugar.

Creamy Pumpkin Soup

Balsamic Chicken

Remember this fast and flavorful chicken entrée when guests drop in. Pictured on page 73.

PER SERVING: 181 cal., 5 g total fat (1 g sat. fat), 66 mg chol., 62 mg sodium, 3 g carb., 1 g fiber, 27 g pro. Exchanges: 4 very lean meat, 1 fat. Carb choices: 0.

- 4 small skinless, boneless chicken breast halves (1 to $1^{1}/4$ pounds total)
- 1 tablespoon olive oil
- 1 tablespoon paprika
- $1/2$ teaspoon snipped fresh rosemary
- 2 cloves garlic, minced
- $1/4$ teaspoon ground black pepper
- Nonstick cooking spray
- $1/4$ cup dry red wine or water
- 3 tablespoons balsamic vinegar
- Fresh rosemary sprigs (optional)

1. If desired, place chicken breast halves between two pieces of plastic wrap. Pound with flat side of a meat mallet to $1/4$- to $1/2$-inch thickness.

2. Stir together oil, paprika, rosemary, garlic, and pepper to form a paste; rub paste onto chicken. Coat a 13×9×2-inch baking pan with cooking spray. Arrange chicken in pan; cover and chill for 2 to 6 hours.

3. Preheat oven to 450°F. Drizzle wine onto chicken. Bake for 10 to 12 minutes or until an instant-read meat thermometer inserted in the thickest portion of the chicken registers 170°F and juices run clear, turning pieces once halfway through cooking. (For pounded chicken, bake about 6 minutes or until chicken is no longer pink and juices run clear, turning the pieces once halfway through cooking.)

4. Remove chicken from oven. Immediately drizzle vinegar onto the chicken in the pan. Transfer chicken to plates. Stir the liquid in the baking pan; drizzle onto the chicken. If desired, garnish with fresh rosemary. Makes 4 servings.

Mock Noodle Kugel

Spaghetti squash makes a great low-carb alternative to pasta in this version of traditional kugel.
Pictured on page 73.

PER SERVING: 75 cal., 4 g total fat (1 g sat. fat), 53 mg chol., 122 mg sodium, 8 g carb., 0 g fiber, 3 g pro. Exchanges: 1.5 vegetable, 0.5 fat. Carb choices: 0.5

  Nonstick cooking spray
1 2¹/2- to 3-pound spaghetti squash
1 tablespoon olive oil
1 medium onion, chopped
2 cloves garlic, minced
2 eggs, lightly beaten*
2 egg whites, lightly beaten*
¹/4 teaspoon salt
  Dash ground black pepper

1. Preheat oven to 375°F. Lightly coat a 1¹/2-quart casserole with cooking spray; set aside.

2. Cut the spaghetti squash in half lengthwise; remove seeds and strings. Place one half of the squash, cut side down, in a microwave-safe baking dish. Using a fork, prick the skin all over.

3. Microwave the spaghetti squash on 100 percent power (high) for 6 to 7 minutes or until tender; carefully remove squash from baking dish. Repeat with the other spaghetti squash half. (Or place both squash halves, cut sides down, in a shallow baking pan and bake at 375°F about 40 minutes or until tender.) Let the squash cool in the pan on a wire rack until it's easy to handle.

4. Meanwhile, in a medium skillet, heat oil over medium heat. Add onion and garlic; cook and stir about 5 minutes or until the onion starts to brown, stirring occasionally.

5. Use a fork to scrape flesh from spaghetti squash halves, holding squash with hot pads if necessary. Place the shredded squash in a large bowl. Cool slightly.

6. Add onion mixture, eggs, egg whites, salt, and pepper to shredded squash. Stir with a wooden spoon. Pour squash mixture into the prepared casserole.

7. Bake kugel about 35 minutes or until set near the center. Cool for 15 minutes on a wire rack. Serve warm. (The kugel may water out slightly when cut.) Makes 8 (about ¹/2-cup) servings.

Sweet Kugel: Prepare Mock Noodle Kugel as directed through Step 3. Omit the oil, onion, garlic, and pepper. Instead, to the shredded spaghetti squash, stir in ¹/4 cup sugar or sugar substitute** equivalent to ¹/4 cup sugar, 1 teaspoon ground cinnamon, and the salt. Continue baking as directed in Step 7.

PER SERVING: 79 cal., 2 g total fat (1 g sat. fat), 53 mg chol., 121 mg sodium, 14 g carb., 0 g fiber, 3 g pro. Exchanges: 1.5 vegetable, 0.5 carb. Carb choices: 1.

PER SERVING WITH SUBSTITUTE: same as above, except 55 cal., 8 g carb. Exchanges: 0 fat, 0 carb. Carb choices: 0.5.

*Test Kitchen Tip: If you like, substitute ³/4 cup refrigerated or thawed egg product for the whole eggs and egg whites.

Sugar Substitutes: Choose from Splenda granular or Sweet'N Low bulk or packets. Follow the package directions to the use product amount that's equivalent to ¹/4 cup sugar.

Quick Tip

When you use flavor-packed ingredients, the result tastes delicious without a lot of sodium, fat, or calories. Rely on additions such as garlic (roasted and unroasted), ground spices, fresh herbs, and vinegars (balsamic, flavored, and rice vinegars), just to name a few.

Creamy Cranberry Salad
recipe, page 80

Creole Turkey Meatballs
recipe, page 80

When Jo Ann Pegues (right photo, far right) teaches nutrition and cooking classes to Denver-area church members, everyone gets involved in making the recipes.

learning together

Where there's faith, there's a foundation for learning—so the Metro Denver Black Church Initiative has discovered. For more than 10 years, this association of more than 40 African-American churches has reached out to members with messages on living healthfully. Jo Ann Pegues, R.D., M.P.A., who is project manager of the initiative's Focus on Diabetes, conducts diabetes cooking classes as part of the program. "People come from all walks of life," Pegues says. "Some have had diabetes for years, some have just been diagnosed, some are at risk, and others are caregivers. Husbands and wives attend together to learn new ways to cook. We love it when ministers join us, because the congregation is likely to follow. There's nothing like preaching from the pulpit to encourage people to make changes!"

The classes are held where members can easily find them—in local Denver-area churches. Attendees learn about other aspects of diabetes care, especially the importance of exercise in relation to diabetes. "In the winter, we've noticed people really slack off," Pegues says. "To show them how easy it is, every class includes 15 to 20 minutes of exercise." Then it's time for students to roll up their sleeves and start cooking. Classes are very hands-on. Everyone steps up to the plate. It's a low-key time to gather around the counter for some chopping, mixing, learning, and laughing. "It's a social thing as well as a learning experience," Pegues says. "That's a key to our success."

"It's a social thing as well as a learning experience. That's a key to our success."

—Jo Ann Pegues, Focus on Diabetes
project manager, Denver

Broccoli and Cauliflower Sauté
recipe, page 80

Broccoli and Cauliflower Sauté

These colorful veggies are low in calories and carbs.
Pictured on page 79.

PER SERVING: 47 cal., 2 g total fat (0 g sat. fat), 0 mg chol., 88 mg sodium, 4 g carb., 1 g fiber, 1 g pro. Exchanges: 1 vegetable, 0.5 fat. Carb choices: 1.

2 teaspoons olive oil
1 cup broccoli florets
1 cup cauliflower florets
1 clove garlic, thinly sliced
1/4 cup dry white wine or reduced-sodium chicken broth
3 tablespoons water
1/8 teaspoon salt
1/8 teaspoon ground black pepper

1. In a large skillet, heat oil over medium-high heat. Add broccoli, cauliflower, and garlic; cook for 2 minutes, stirring occasionally. Carefully add wine, the water, salt, and pepper; reduce heat to low.
2. Cover and cook for 2 minutes. Uncover; increase heat to medium. Cook for 2 minutes or until vegetables are tender. Makes 4 (1/2-cup) servings.

Creamy Cranberry Salad

Raspberries combine with cranberries in this pretty salad.
Pictured on page 78.

PER SERVING: 118 cal., 7 g total fat (4 g sat. fat), 22 mg chol., 118 mg sodium, 11 g carb., 1 g fiber, 4 g pro. Exchanges: 1 other carb., 1 fat. Carb choices: 1.

1 envelope unflavored gelatin
2 teaspoons sugar
1 cup fresh or frozen raspberries, thawed
1/2 cup canned whole cranberry sauce
1 8-ounce package reduced-fat cream cheese (Neufchâtel), softened
1/2 cup low-calorie cranberry juice
1/4 cup chopped pecans, toasted (optional)
   Sugared cranberries* (optional)
   Sugared fresh basil leaves* (optional)

1. In a small saucepan, stir together the gelatin and sugar. Stir in 1/2 cup *water*. Cook and stir over medium-low heat until gelatin dissolves; set aside.
2. In a large bowl, mash raspberries and cranberry sauce with a potato masher until coarsely mashed. Add cream cheese; beat with an electric mixer on low to medium speed until well combined. Gradually beat in cranberry juice until combined.
3. Stir gelatin mixture and, if desired, pecans into cranberry mixture. Divide mixture among eight 4-ounce stainless steel** gelatin molds or 4-ounce ramekins, or pour into a 1 1/2-quart glass dish. Cover and chill for at least 4 hours or until firm. Unmold onto individual serving plates if using individual molds. If desired, garnish with sugared cranberries and basil. Makes 8 servings.

*Test Kitchen Tip: To make sugared cranberries and basil leaves, sprinkle berries and leaves with water. Roll in granulated sugar, turning to coat evenly.

**Note: It is important to use molds that are not aluminum to avoid a reaction with the acidic gelatin mixture.

Creole Turkey Meatballs

Look for ground turkey breast to keep the meatballs
low in fat. Pictured on page 78.

PER SERVING: 94 cal., 4 g total fat (1 g sat. fat), 36 mg chol., 104 mg sodium, 5 g carb., 1 g fiber, 9 g pro. Exchanges: 0.5 other carb., 1 lean meat. Carb choices: 0.

   Nonstick cooking spray
1/4 cup refrigerated or frozen egg product, thawed, or 1 egg
1 medium onion, chopped
1 medium green sweet pepper, chopped
1/2 cup quick-cooking rolled oats
2 tablespoons fat-free milk
2 cloves garlic, minced
1 teaspoon dried Italian seasoning, crushed
1 teaspoon salt-free seasoning
1 teaspoon Creole seasoning
1 pound uncooked ground turkey

1. Preheat oven to 375°F. Lightly coat a 15×10×1-inch baking pan with cooking spray; set aside.
2. In a large bowl, beat egg; stir in onion, pepper, oats, milk, and garlic. Stir in Italian, salt-free, and Creole seasonings. Add turkey; mix well.
3. Using a rounded tablespoon, shape mixture into 1 1/4-inch balls. Arrange in prepared pan.
4. Bake meatballs, uncovered, about 25 minutes or until brown and no longer pink in center (165°F). Makes 10 servings.

Citrus-Sweet Potato Pie

Using oil instead of lard in the crust lowers
the saturated fat in this pumpkinlike pie.

PER SERVING: 172 cal., 6 g total fat (1 g sat. fat), 1 mg chol.,
96 mg sodium, 25 g carb., 1 g fiber, 4 g pro. Exchanges: 1 starch,
0.5 other carb., 1 fat. Carb choices: 1.5.

PER SERVING WITH SUBSTITUTE: same as above, except 157 cal.,
21 g carb.

1½ cups mashed, cooked, peeled sweet potatoes (about
    2 medium)
¼   cup sugar or sugar substitute* equivalent to
    ¼ cup sugar
1   teaspoon vanilla
½   teaspoon finely shredded lemon peel
1   teaspoon lemon juice
¼   teaspoon ground nutmeg
¼   cup refrigerated or frozen egg product, thawed,
    or 1 egg
1   cup evaporated fat-free milk
1   recipe Baked Oil Pastry (see recipe, right)
    Frozen fat-free whipped dessert topping, thawed
    (optional)
    Ground nutmeg (optional)

1. Preheat oven to 350°F. For filling, in a large bowl,
stir together sweet potatoes, sugar, vanilla, lemon peel,
lemon juice, and the ¼ teaspoon nutmeg. Add egg. Beat
gently with a fork just until combined. Gradually add
evaporated milk; stir until combined.

2. Pour filling into Baked Oil Pastry. To prevent
overbrowning, cover edge with foil. Bake for 30 to
35 minutes or until a knife inserted near the center
comes out clean and edges are puffed. If necessary to
allow pastry to brown, remove foil for the last 5 to
10 minutes of baking. Cool on a wire rack. Cover and
refrigerate within 2 hours.

3. To serve, remove tart from pan or leave pie in pie
plate. Cut into wedges. If desired, top each serving with
topping and additional nutmeg. Makes 12 servings.

Baked Oil Pastry: Preheat oven to 450°F. In a medium
bowl, stir together 1⅓ cups all-purpose flour and
¼ teaspoon salt. Add ⅓ cup cooking oil and 3 tablespoons
fat-free milk all at once. Stir gently with a fork. Form
into a ball. On a well-floured surface, slightly flatten
dough. Roll from center to edge into an 11-inch circle.
To transfer, wrap pastry around the rolling pin. Unroll
into 9-inch tart pan with a removable bottom or a 9-inch
pie plate. Ease pastry into pan without stretching. Press
pastry into fluted sides of tart pan or crimp edge in pie
plate, trimming pastry as needed. Line pastry with a
double thickness of foil. Bake for 8 minutes. Remove foil.
Bake for 5 minutes more. Cool on a wire rack.

***Sugar Substitutes:** Choose from Splenda granular or
Sweet 'N Low bulk or packets. Follow package directions
to use product amount equivalent to ¼ cup sugar.

**Peach-Berry
Frozen Dessert**
recipe, page 85

Jill's son, Lucas, burst into tears
when they couldn't go to his favorite
drive-through because it wasn't a
healthful choice for Jill. "He thought
we'd never eat burgers and fries
again," Jill says. "We had to make
changes in how we ate as a family,
not just for us but for our kids."

(jill waage)

breaking the pattern

**With diabetes running in her family, Jill Waage didn't
want her children to hear the same diagnosis that
she and her father had.** So with the help of her husband, Jerry,
Jill embarked on a lifestyle improvement program to break the
family chain of diabetes.

Jill's grandmother and father both had type 2 diabetes. And after
the birth of daughter, Eliza, Jill found out she had pre-diabetes.
"Since I had gestational diabetes, I expected it," she says. "But I was
shocked that it happened so soon." She already knew how diabetes
can affect a whole family. "I remember when Dad found out in his
early 40s. Mom changed the way she cooked," Jill recalls.

Thanks to her parents, Jill, knew the kind of adjustments she had
to make. But how would her young family react? "We had to make
changes in how we ate as a family, not just for us but for our kids,"
Jill acknowledges.

Jill and Jerry, who live in Urbandale, Iowa, discussed what they
ate and how they could still enjoy food but make it more healthful.
They also wanted everyone to eat the same thing—no special meals
for Jill. "Overnight, I became the biggest label reader. I check carbs
and look for whole grains," she says. "We eat a lot of vegetables,
steaming them just until they're barely tender—the kids love them
that way, especially edamame (fresh soybeans). I've learned how to
flavor with spices and herbs and citrus.

"So much more is available today than when Mom started
cooking for Dad 30 years ago," Jill continues. "Back then, her motto
was 'Leave it out and do without.' Now we have low-carb ingredients
and easy ways to adapt our favorite foods."

The kids have learned that diabetes doesn't mean doing
without treats, just having them at times and in amounts that are
appropriate. Her son knows that if he's hungry after dessert, it's
healthful food time. "Now he'll even tell me he's hungry and ask for
a 'healthy snack,'" Jill marvels.

"In many cases, I already had some great recipes. I just looked at how I could cut the fat and carbs."

—Jill Waage,
Urbandale, Iowa

Smoked Brisket with Zesty Barbecue Sauce, Blue Cheese Coleslaw
recipes, pages 84 and 85

Ginger Ale Salad

Smoked Brisket with Zesty Barbecue Sauce

Wine mop sauce, black pepper rub, and a kicky barbecue sauce flavor the smoked meat. Pictured on page 83.

PER SERVING: 232 cal., 10 g total fat (3 g sat. fat), 73 mg chol., 535 mg sodium, 8 g carb., 1 g fiber, 25 g pro. Exchanges: 0.5 other carb., 3.5 lean meat. Carb choices: 0.5.

- 8 to 10 mesquite or hickory wood chunks
- 1/4 cup dry red wine or reduced-sodium beef broth
- 4 teaspoons Worcestershire sauce
- 1 tablespoon cooking oil
- 1 tablespoon red wine vinegar or cider vinegar
- 1 clove garlic, minced
- 1/2 teaspoon coriander seeds, crushed
- 1/2 teaspoon hot-style mustard
-    Dash cayenne pepper
- 1 teaspoon seasoned salt
- 1 teaspoon paprika
- 1 teaspoon ground black pepper
- 1 3- to 3 1/2-pound fresh beef brisket
- 1 recipe Zesty Barbecue Sauce (see recipe, below)

1. At least 1 hour before cooking, soak wood chunks in enough water to cover. Drain wood before using.

2. For mop sauce, in a small bowl, combine wine, Worcestershire sauce, oil, vinegar, garlic, coriander seeds, mustard, and cayenne. Set aside.

3. For rub, in a small bowl, combine seasoned salt, paprika, and black pepper.

4. Trim most of the visible fat from meat. Sprinkle rub mixture evenly onto the meat; rub in with your fingers.

5. In a smoker, arrange preheated coals, wood chunks, and water pan according to the manufacturer's directions. Pour water into pan.

6. Place meat on grill rack over water pan. Cover and smoke for 5 to 6 hours or until meat is tender, brushing once or twice with mop sauce during last 1 hour of smoking. Add additional coals, wood chunks, and water as needed to maintain temperature and smoke. Discard any remaining mop sauce.

7. To serve, thinly slice meat across the grain. Serve sliced meat with Zesty Barbecue Sauce. Makes 8 (3-ounce) servings.

Zesty Barbecue Sauce: Coat an unheated small saucepan with nonstick cooking spray. Preheat over medium heat. Add 1/2 cup chopped green sweet pepper, 2 tablespoons chopped onion, and 1 minced clove garlic; cook and stir about 5 minutes or until tender. Stir in 1/2 cup ketchup;

Ginger Ale Salad

A double-ginger whammy of crystallized ginger and ginger ale makes this salad a standout at your holiday meal.

PER SERVING: 50 cal., 0 g total fat (0 g sat. fat), 0 mg chol., 63 mg sodium, 11 g carb., 1 g fiber, 1 g pro. Exchanges: 1.5 other carb. Carb choices: 1.

- 1 6-ounce package sugar-free, low-calorie lemon-flavored gelatin
- 1 cup water
- 2 cups diet ginger ale
- 2 cups assorted chopped fruit (such as drained canned pineapple [do not use fresh pineapple], fresh strawberries; fresh or canned peaches or pears; fresh apple; or fresh grapes)
- 1/2 cup sliced celery or chopped toasted nuts
- 2 tablespoons finely chopped crystallized ginger
-    Frozen whipped dessert topping thawed (optional)
-    Chopped nuts, toasted (optional)

1. In a medium saucepan, combine gelatin and water; heat and stir until gelatin dissolves. Stir in ginger ale. Chill about 30 minutes or until partially set (the consistency of unbeaten egg whites). Fold in fruit, celery, and crystallized ginger.

2. Pour into a 6-cup mold. Cover and chill about 6 hours or until firm. Unmold salad onto a serving plate. Makes 12 servings.

1 large tomato, peeled, seeded, and chopped; 1 tablespoon steak sauce; 1 tablespoon Worcestershire sauce; 1 teaspoon brown sugar; $\frac{1}{4}$ teaspoon ground cinnamon; $\frac{1}{8}$ teaspoon ground nutmeg; $\frac{1}{8}$ teaspoon ground cloves; $\frac{1}{8}$ teaspoon ground ginger; and $\frac{1}{8}$ teaspoon ground black pepper. Bring to boiling; reduce heat. Cover and simmer for 5 minutes. Serve warm or cool. Makes about $1\frac{3}{4}$ cups.

Peach-Berry Frozen Dessert

Fat-free cheese, yogurt, and light dessert topping keep this low in calories, carbs, and fat. Pictured on page 82.

PER SERVING: 89 cal., 2 g total fat (2 g sat. fat), 3 mg chol., 159 mg sodium, 12 g carb., 1 g fiber, 6 g pro. Exchanges: 1 other carb., 1 very lean meat. Carb choices: 1.

  1 8-ounce package fat-free cream cheese, softened
  2 6-ounce cartons peach fat-free yogurt with sweetener
$\frac{1}{2}$ of an 8-ounce container frozen light whipped dessert topping, thawed
  1 cup chopped, pitted, peeled fresh peaches; frozen unsweetened peach slices, thawed, drained, and chopped; or one 8.25-ounce can peach slices (juice pack), drained and chopped
  1 cup fresh or frozen unsweetened blueberries, raspberries, and/or strawberries, thawed and drained if frozen
     Fresh mint leaves (optional)
     Fresh berries (optional)

1. In a medium bowl, combine the cream cheese and yogurt. Beat with an electric mixer on medium speed until smooth. Fold in the whipped topping, peaches, and the 1 cup berries.

2. Pour berry mixture into a 2-quart square baking dish. Cover and freeze about 8 hours or until mixture is firm.

3. To serve, let dessert stand at room temperature about 45 minutes to thaw slightly. Cut into squares. If desired, garnish with fresh mint leaves and additional berries. Makes 9 ($\frac{1}{2}$-cup) servings.

Make-Ahead Directions: Prepare the dessert as directed in Step 1; cover and freeze for up to 1 week.

Quick Tip

Choosing lower-fat dairy products makes good sense. But sometimes, a product you love, such as some cheeses, might not be available in low-fat form. Blue cheese, sharp cheddar, and Gruyére pack a big punch of flavor. So just use a small amount.

Blue Cheese Coleslaw

You can substitute broccoli slaw mix for the coleslaw mix. Pictured on page 83.

PER SERVING: 95 cal., 8 g total fat (1 g sat. fat), 3 mg chol., 115 mg sodium, 5 g carb., 1 g fiber, 1 g pro. Exchanges: 0.5 vegetable, 1.5 fat. Carb choices: 0.

$\frac{1}{2}$ cup cider vinegar or rice vinegar
$\frac{1}{3}$ cup canola oil or salad oil
  1 tablespoon sugar
  1 teaspoon dry mustard
$\frac{1}{2}$ teaspoon onion powder
$\frac{1}{4}$ teaspoon salt
$\frac{1}{4}$ teaspoon ground white or black pepper
  1 16-ounce package (5 cups) shredded cabbage with carrot (coleslaw mix)
$\frac{1}{4}$ cup crumbled blue cheese (1 ounce)

1. For dressing, in a screw-top jar, combine vinegar, oil, sugar, mustard, onion powder, salt, and pepper. Cover and shake well to mix. Chill the dressing until ready to serve.

2. Before serving, in a large bowl, combine shredded cabbage and blue cheese. Shake dressing; pour over cabbage mixture. Gently toss cabbage mixture to coat. Makes 10 ($\frac{1}{2}$-cup) servings.

Make-Ahead Directions: Prepare the dressing through Step 1. Cover and refrigerate for up to 1 week.

party-perfect
appetizers

Dried Cranberry
Chutney Appetizers

Preparing for a party can be a lot of fun. Menu choices, however, can be difficult when you have diabetes. To help you celebrate, we've taken the stress out of planning a festive gathering. These appetizers not only taste great but will fit your meal plan, too.

Dried Cranberry Chutney Appetizers

Just four ingredients added to purchased chutney make taste buds tingle with delight. Serve a spoonful on apple or pear wedges for a fat-free snack.

PER SERVING: 37 cal., 0 g total fat (0 g sat. fat), 0 mg chol., 2 mg sodium, 9 g carb., 0 g fiber, 0 g pro. Exchanges: 0.5 fruit. Carb choices: 0.5.

1/2 **cup dried cranberries**
1/4 **cup water**
2 **tablespoons sugar**
1 **tablespoon finely chopped fresh ginger**
3/4 **cup mango chutney**
Fat-free cream cheese
Apple slices
Toasted baguette slices or crackers

1. In a small saucepan, combine dried cranberries, water, sugar, and ginger. Bring to boiling. Cover and remove from heat. Let stand for 15 minutes.
2. Snip any large pieces of mango chutney. Stir the chutney into cranberry mixture. Cover and chill for at least 2 hours.
3. Serve the chutney with cream cheese, apple slices, and baguette slices. Makes 22 (1-tablespoon) servings.

(how much is enough?)

The number of appetizers you need for your party will depend upon the number of guests, the types of appetizers you'll be serving, and the time of day. Appetites will be greater if it's close to dinnertime than they will be at a late-evening function. If a full dinner follows your appetizers, guests will eat about half of what they would at an all-appetizer party. For cocktail parties, plan on about 12 bite-size servings per person. Hot appetizers and shrimp generally go fast, so make plenty!

Greek Layer Dip

Curried Carrot Spread

Greek Layer Dip

Purchased hummus, a Middle-Eastern dip, makes this an easy dish to prepare. Look for containers of hummus in supermarkets near the better-quality cheeses.

PER SERVING: 120 cal., 4 g total fat (1 g sat. fat), 6 mg chol., 231 mg sodium, 17 g carb., 2 g fiber, 5 g pro. Exchanges: 1 starch, 0.5 fat. Carb choices: 1.

- 1 cup plain low-fat yogurt
- ¼ cup coarsely shredded unpeeled cucumber
- 1 tablespoon finely chopped red onion
- 1 teaspoon snipped fresh mint
- 1 8-ounce container (³/₄ cup) plain hummus
- ½ cup chopped, seeded tomato
- 2 ounces feta cheese, crumbled (¹/₂ cup)
  Chopped cucumber (optional)
  Sliced green onion (optional)
- 3 large white and/or wheat pita bread rounds

1. In a small bowl, stir together the yogurt, shredded cucumber, red onion, and mint. Set aside.

2. Spread hummus in the bottom of a 10-inch quiche dish or 9-inch pie plate. Spread yogurt mixture over hummus. Sprinkle with tomato and feta cheese. If desired, top with cucumber and green onion.

3. Split each pita bread round in half, making 2 rounds; cut each round into 8 wedges.* Serve pita bread wedges with dip. Makes 10 (¹/₄-cup) servings.

***Test Kitchen Tip:** For crispier pita bread dippers, spread wedges in a single layer on baking sheets. Lightly sprinkle with water. Sprinkle wedges with paprika and crushed dried oregano. Bake in a 350°F oven about 10 minutes or until crisp. Cool; cover and store in a cool, dry place.

Curried Carrot Spread

This brightly hued spread is full of good-for-you ingredients. Cumin adds a zippy backround flavor.

PER SERVING: 40 cal., 1 g total fat (0 g sat. fat), 0 mg chol., 84 mg sodium, 6 g carb., 2 g fiber, 2 g pro. Exchanges: 0.5 starch. Carb choices: 0.5.

- 3 cups sliced carrots
- ³/₄ cup chopped onion
- 3 cloves garlic, minced
- 2 tablespoons olive oil or cooking oil
- 1 tablespoon curry powder
- 1 teaspoon ground cumin
- 1 15-ounce can white kidney (cannellini) beans, rinsed and drained
- ³/₄ teaspoon salt
  Thinly sliced green onion (optional)
  Crackers or vegetable dippers

1. In a covered medium saucepan, cook carrots in a small amount of boiling water about 15 minutes or until very tender. Drain.

2. Meanwhile, in a small skillet, cook onion and garlic in hot oil until tender. Stir in curry powder and cumin. Transfer carrots and onion mixture to a food processor; add white kidney beans and salt. Cover and process until smooth. Transfer to a serving bowl; cover and chill for 4 hours to 3 days

3. If using, garnish with green onion. Serve with crackers, melba toast, toasted French bread slices, or vegetable dippers. Makes 48 (2-tablespoon) servings.

(surefire party tips)

Consider these planning tips:

1. **Select** interesting foods to serve. Be creative and don't stick to just one cuisine.
2. **Offer** an assortment. For small gatherings of 8 to 10 guests, three or four types of appetizers are suitable; for parties of up to 45 guests, plan on six; and for more than 45 guests, offer eight types.
3. **Plan** appetizers from each of the following categories: meat or poultry, fish or seafood, cheese, and vegetables or fruit.
4. **Consider** serving hearty appetizers if the party spans several hours. For example, meatballs, meat kabobs, or those made with bread.
5. **Think** visual appeal. Combine foods with interesting color contrasts and texture.
6. **Serve** party-friendly foods that aren't messy or greasy, are easy to pick up quickly, and are substantial enough to be eaten with two fingers.
7. **Offer** drink choices such as wine and beer or stick to champagne or one specialty drink such as margaritas or a punch bowl of eggnog.
8. **Provide** a variety of nonalcoholic options for nondrinkers and designated drivers.
9. **Supplement** your own appetizers with selections from a gourmet shop and/or cheeses, fruits, and nuts.

Creamy Dried-Tomato Spread

Creamy Dried-Tomato Spread

Goat cheese and cream cheese give this spread its creamy consistency. Dried tomato and basil supply the flavor.

PER SERVING: 67 cal., 5 g total fat (3 g sat. fat), 14 mg chol., 126 mg sodium, 2 g carb., 0 g fiber, 4 g pro. Exchanges: 0.5 medium-fat meat 0.5 fat. Carb choices: 0.

- $1/3$ cup dried tomatoes (not oil-packed)
  Boiling water
- 4 ounces soft goat cheese (chèvre)
- $1/2$ of an 8-ounce package reduced-fat cream cheese (Neufchâtel), softened
- $1/4$ cup snipped fresh basil or 2 teaspoons dried basil, crushed
- 3 cloves garlic, minced
- $1/8$ teaspoon ground black pepper
- 2 to 3 tablespoons fat-free milk
  Miniature toasts and/or assorted reduced-fat crackers

1. In a small bowl, cover dried tomatoes with boiling water; let stand for 10 minutes. Drain tomatoes, discarding liquid. Finely snip tomatoes.

2. In a medium bowl, stir together snipped tomatoes, goat cheese, cream cheese, basil, garlic, and pepper. Stir in enough of the milk to make spreading consistency. Cover and chill for at least 2 hours or up to 8 hours. Serve spread with miniature toasts and/or crackers. Makes 10 (2-tablespoon) servings.

Crab and Vegetable Roll-Ups

When using wasabi, known as Japanese horseradish, a little goes a long way. Add more only with discretion.

PER ROLL-UP: 23 cal., 2 g total fat (0 g sat. fat), 4 mg chol., 37 mg sodium, 1 g carb., 1 g fiber, 1 g pro. Exchanges: 0.5 fat. Carb choices: 0.

- 2 medium zucchini or yellow summer squash
- $1/2$ cup cooked lump crabmeat
- 1 tablespoon mayonnaise or salad dressing
- 1 teaspoon wasabi paste
- $1/8$ teaspoon salt
- $1/2$ of a medium avocado
- 2 tablespoons coarsely shredded carrot
- 16 small fresh basil leaves
- 8 canned mandarin orange sections
  Reduced-sodium soy sauce (optional)

1. Trim ends of zucchini. Using a sharp vegetable peeler, slice zucchini lengthwise into wide, flat ribbons. Discard first and last slices and the seedy portions in the middle. (You will need 32 ribbons.) Set zucchini ribbons aside.

2. Carefully clean crabmeat, removing any shell or cartilage pieces. Drain crabmeat well in a colander, pressing with the back of a spoon to remove most of the liquid. Pat dry with paper towels.

3. In a small bowl, combine crabmeat, mayonnaise, wasabi paste, and salt. Seed and peel the avocado; cut into thin strips.

4. On a clean work surface, place one zucchini ribbon on top of another. For each roll-up, place 1 slightly rounded teaspoon of crab mixture at one end of a doubled zucchini ribbon. Top with avocado strips, a few shreds of carrot, and a basil leaf. Roll up; secure with toothpicks. If desired, cover and chill for up to 30 minutes. Makes 16 roll-ups.

Crab and Vegetable Roll-Ups

Quick Tip:

If you're planning to arrange appetizers on a buffet table, have a center of interest, such as an elegant appetizer or a centerpiece. Place other plates of food around it. A pretty savory tart set on a lovely cake pedestal would be a perfect eye-grabber.

Herb-Stuffed Cherry Tomatoes

Herb-Stuffed Cherry Tomatoes

These bright bite-size gems are easy to make. Prepare them up to 2 hours in advance, then cover and refrigerate until serving time.

PER TOMATO: 40 cal., 3 g total fat (2 g sat. fat), 8 mg chol., 38 mg sodium, 1 g carb., 0 g fiber, 1 g pro. Exchanges: 1 fat. Carb choices: 0.

- 3 dozen cherry tomatoes, 1 to 1½ inches in diameter
- 2 tablespoons purchased pesto
- 1 clove garlic, minced
- 2 tablespoons snipped fresh parsley
- 2 tablespoons snipped fresh chives
- 1 tablespoon snipped fresh tarragon or dill
- 1 8-ounce package reduced-fat cream cheese
- 4 ounces fresh goat cheese (chèvre)
  Fresh parsley or fresh dill sprigs (optional)
  Cucumber slices (optional)

1. Using a sharp knife, cut off the top third of each tomato on the stem end. Set aside the tops for garnish, if desired, or discard. Hollow out tomatoes; invert on paper towels and set aside.

2. Place pesto, garlic, the 2 tablespoons parsley, chives, and tarragon or dill in a food processor. Process for 15 seconds; add the cream cheese and chèvre. Process another 30 to 45 seconds or until the filling is smooth.

3. Place the filling in a pastry bag fitted with a star tip and pipe into each cherry tomato. If desired, place each tomato on a cucumber slice. Garnish with fresh parsley or dill sprigs and/or reserved tomato tops. Makes 36 stuffed tomatoes.

Mozzarella with Basil

Reinvent this recipe every time you make it by varying the cheese and herb. Try feta with oregano or dill, or queso fresco with cumin or red pepper flakes.

PER SERVING: 88 cal., 6 g total fat (3 g sat. fat), 18 mg chol., 176 mg sodium, 1 g carb., 0 g fiber, 7 g pro. Exchanges: 1 lean meat, 0.5 fat. Carb choices: 0.

- 1 pound part-skim mozzarella cheese
- 2 tablespoons roasted garlic oil or olive oil
- 1 to 2 teaspoons balsamic vinegar
- 2 tablespoons snipped fresh basil or 1 teaspoon dried basil, crushed
- 1 tablespoon freshly cracked black pepper
  Tomato slices (optional)
  Fresh basil strips (optional)
  Baguette-style French bread slices, toasted (optional)

1. Cut mozzarella into ½-inch pieces. Place pieces in a medium bowl. In a small bowl combine oil, vinegar, snipped basil, and pepper. Pour over cheese; toss gently until cheese is well coated. Cover and chill for 1 hour.

2. If desired, serve with tomato, basil strips, and bread slices. Makes 16 servings.

Make-Ahead Directions: Prepare as above through Step 1. Store, covered, in the refrigerator up to 3 days. To serve, let stand at room temperature until olive oil liquefies. If desired, serve with tomato, basil strips, and bread slices.

Deviled Eggs with Curried Crab

1. Halve the hard-cooked eggs lengthwise and remove yolks. Set whites aside. In a quart-size resealable plastic bag, place egg yolks, $1/4$ cup mayonnaise dressing, the green onion, mustard, $1/8$ teaspoon salt, and $1/8$ teaspoon cayenne pepper. Seal bag. Gently squeeze the bag to combine ingredients. Snip off one corner of the bag; pipe egg yolk mixture into egg white halves. (Or in a small bowl, combine yolks, the $1/4$ cup mayonnaise dressing, the green onion, mustard, $1/8$ teaspoon of the salt, and $1/8$ teaspoon cayenne pepper; mash and stir with a fork until well mixed. Spoon into a decorating bag fitted with a star tip; pipe into egg white halves.)

2. Cut up any large pieces of chutney. In a small bowl, combine 3 tablespoons mayonnaise dressing, the chutney, curry powder, remaining $1/8$ teaspoon salt, and remaining $1/8$ teaspoon cayenne pepper. Gently fold in crabmeat. Top each deviled egg with a spoonful of the crab mixture. Cover and chill for at least 1 hour or up to 2 hours. If desired, garnish with one or more of the suggested garnishes. Makes 16 appetizers.

Make-Ahead Directions: The egg yolk mixture may be made a day ahead and stored, covered, in the refrigerator. Wrap and store egg white halves separately.

Deviled Eggs with Curried Crab

These upscale deviled eggs take about 20 minutes to make and can be chilled for up to 2 hours.

PER APPETIZER: 70 cal., 5 g total fat (1 g sat. fat), 113 mg chol., 142 mg sodium, 2 g carb., 0 g fiber, 4 g pro. Exchanges: 0.5 medium-fat meat, 0.5 fat. Carb choices: 0.

- 8 hard-cooked eggs
- $1/4$ cup light mayonnaise dressing or salad dressing
- 1 tablespoon finely chopped green onion
- 1 to 2 teaspoons flavored mustard (such as **Dijon**-style mustard or horseradish mustard)
- $1/4$ teaspoon salt
- $1/4$ teaspoon cayenne pepper
- 3 tablespoons light mayonnaise dressing or salad dressing
- 1 to 2 tablespoons purchased mango chutney
- $1/2$ teaspoon curry powder
- $1/2$ cup cooked crabmeat (about $2^3/4$ ounces)
  Suggested garnishes (finely chopped sweet pepper, snipped fresh chives, sliced or chopped toasted almonds, cracked black pepper, or paprika) (optional)

Gorgonzola and Onion Tart

Tarts such as this one make grand centerpieces. Place the tart on a favorite cake pedestal for a nice presentation.

PER SERVING: 214 cal., 11 g total fat (4 g sat. fat), 74 mg chol., 279 mg sodium, 2 g carb., 0 g fiber, 25 g pro. Exchanges: 3.5 lean meat, 0.5 fat. Carb choices: 0.

- Nonstick cooking spray
- $1^1/4$ cups all-purpose flour
- $1/2$ teaspoon dried thyme, chervil, or marjoram, crushed
- $1/4$ teaspoon salt
- $1/4$ cup fat-free milk
- 3 tablespoons cooking oil
- 1 cup thinly sliced onion
- $1/2$ cup shredded zucchini
- $1/2$ cup crumbled **Gorgonzola** or blue cheese (2 ounces)
- 2 egg whites
- 1 egg
- $1/4$ teaspoon ground black pepper
- $1/2$ cup fat-free milk
  Fresh thyme, chervil, or marjoram (optional)
  Apple or pear slices (optional)

1. Preheat oven to 425°F. Lightly coat a 9-inch tart pan with removable sides with cooking spray.

2. For pastry, in a medium bowl, stir together the flour, desired dried herb, and salt. In a 1-cup measure, combine 1/4 cup milk and oil. Add all at once to flour mixture. Stir with a fork. On a lightly floured surface, roll dough from center to edge into an 11-inch circle. Ease into prepared tart pan. Trim pastry even with edge of pan. Do not prick pastry. Line with a double thickness of heavy foil. Press foil down firmly but gently.

3. Bake tart for 5 minutes. Remove foil. Bake for 5 to 7 minutes more or until pastry is nearly done. Remove from oven and place on a wire rack. Reduce oven temperature to 375°F.

4. For filling, cook onion and zucchini in a small amount of boiling water about 5 minutes or until onion is tender. Drain well. In a medium bowl, beat the cheese, egg whites, whole egg, and pepper with an electric mixer on low speed until combined. (Cheese will be lumpy.) Stir in onion mixture and the 1/2 cup milk.

5. Spoon the filling into prebaked tart shell. Bake about 20 minutes or until a knife inserted near the center comes out clean. Cool on a wire rack for 15 minutes. Carefully remove sides of tart pan. Serve warm. If desired, garnish with fresh herb and apple or pear slices. Makes 16 servings.

Spinach-Cheese Tart

Spinach-Cheese Tart

Using oil instead of shortening or butter in the pastry dough keeps saturated fat low. Try a fruity olive oil for added flavor.

PER SERVING: 142 cal., 7 g total fat (3 g sat. fat), 46 mg chol., 112 mg sodium, 12 g carb., 1 g fiber, 6 g pro. Exchanges: 1 starch, 1 lean meat. Carb choices: 1.

1 recipe **Oil Pastry** (see recipe, below)
2 eggs
1 cup light ricotta cheese
1/2 cup crumbled semisoft goat cheese (chèvre)
1/4 cup fat-free milk
1/2 cup chopped spinach
1/4 cup chopped, well-drained bottled roasted red sweet peppers
2 teaspoons snipped fresh oregano or 3/4 teaspoon dried oregano, crushed
  Red and/or yellow sweet pepper strips (optional)
  Fresh oregano sprigs (optional)

1. Preheat oven to 450°F. Prepare Oil Pastry. On a lightly floured surface, roll pastry into a 12-inch circle. Ease into a 9 1/2- or 10-inch tart pan with a removable bottom, being careful not to stretch the pastry. Trim pastry even with rim of pan. Do not prick pastry.

2. Line pastry with a double thickness of foil. Bake pastry for 10 to 12 minutes or until edge is golden brown. Remove from oven. Remove foil. Reduce oven temperature to 325°F.

3. Meanwhile, in a medium bowl, beat eggs slightly with an electric mixer. Add ricotta cheese, goat cheese, and milk; beat until smooth. Stir in spinach, roasted red peppers, and the snipped fresh or dried oregano. Pour egg mixture into tart shell.

4. Bake about 20 minutes or until a knife inserted near the center comes out clean.

5. Let stand about 5 minutes before serving. If desired, top with sweet pepper strips and fresh oregano sprigs. Makes 12 servings.

Oil Pastry: In a medium bowl, stir together 1 1/4 cups all-purpose flour and 1/4 teaspoon salt. In a 1-cup measure combine 1/4 cup fat-free milk and 3 tablespoons cooking oil. Add all at once to the flour mixture. Stir with a fork until dough forms a ball.

Quick Tip:

Convenient products from your local supermarket can shave time off your work in the kitchen. Pizza crust mix, phyllo dough and frozen bread dough are a few examples. You can make them into a variety of delicious appetizers (see recipes, below and right).

Mediterranean Pizzettas

Using a pizza crust mix for these savory bites of cheese and sauce helps to save you time in the kitchen.

PER SERVING: 71 cal., 3 g total fat (1 g sat. fat), 12 mg chol., 155 mg sodium, 7 g carb., 0 g fiber, 5 g pro. Exchanges: 0.5 starch, 0.5 lean meat. Carb choices: 0.5.

- 1 6- or 6^1/$_2$-ounce package pizza crust mix
- 1 14^1/$_2$-ounce can no-salt-added diced tomatoes, drained
- 3 tablespoons no-salt-added tomato paste
- 1 teaspoon dried Italian seasoning, crushed
- 2 cloves garlic, minced
- 2 cups sliced or chopped cooked chicken or turkey
- ^{1}/$_2$ cup pitted green olives and/or pitted kalamata olives, coarsely chopped
- ^{1}/$_4$ cup sliced green onions or chopped onion
- 2 tablespoons sliced almonds and/or pine nuts
- ^{1}/$_2$ cup shredded part-skim mozzarella cheese (2 ounces)
- 1 tablespoon snipped fresh Italian (flat-leaf) parsley

1. Preheat oven to 425°F. Prepare pizza crust according to package directions. Pat dough into a greased 15×10×1-inch baking pan (crust will be thin). Bake for 5 minutes.

2. In a small bowl, combine drained tomatoes, the tomato paste, Italian seasoning, and garlic; spread evenly over crust. Top with chicken, olives, onion, and almonds. Sprinkle with cheese.

3. Bake for 15 minutes or until edges of crust are golden. Remove pizza from oven; sprinkle with parsley. Cut into 12 squares; cut each piece in half diagonally. Makes 24 servings.

Tomato-Rosemary Focaccia

American bakers have made this Italian flatbread a trendy favorite. By starting with frozen bread dough, we've made it easy.

PER SERVING: 111 cal., 2 g total fat (1 g sat. fat), 2 mg chol., 34 mg sodium, 17 g carb., 0 g fiber, 3 g pro. Exchanges: 1 starch, 0.5 fat. Carb choices: 1.

- 1 16-ounce loaf frozen white bread dough, thawed
- ^{1}/$_4$ cup finely shredded mozzarella cheese
- 1 to 2 tablespoons olive or cooking oil
- 1 clove garlic, minced
- ^{1}/$_8$ teaspoon ground black pepper
- 1 medium tomato, peeled, seeded, and chopped
- ^{1}/$_4$ cup freshly grated Parmesan cheese (1 ounce)
- 1 tablespoon snipped fresh rosemary or 1 teaspoon dried rosemary, crushed

1. Preheat oven to 400°F. On lightly floured surface, shape bread dough into ball. Cover and let rest for 5 minutes. Roll dough into 14-inch circle. Transfer dough to greased 12-inch pizza pan. Sprinkle with mozzarella cheese. Bake about 15 minutes or until golden and crusty. Cool to room temperature.

2. In small bowl, stir together oil, garlic, and pepper; brush over bread. Sprinkle with tomato, Parmesan cheese, and rosemary.

3. Bake for 10 to 15 minutes more or until focaccia is heated through and cheese is melted. Cut into serving-size pieces. Makes 12 servings.

Make-Ahead Directions: Prepare crust, cool, and store in an airtight container in refrigerator for up to 1 day. Just before serving, add toppings and bake.

Tomato-Rosemary Focaccia

(do-it-yourself party)

Some hosts like to involve their guests in do-it-yourself serving by setting out the makings for snacks or appetizers, such as mini tacos or quesadillas, and letting the guests put together their own dishes to their liking. It makes preparation easier for the host and encourages guests to mingle and get better acquainted or to catch up with old friends.

Walnut-Olive Quesadillas

These Mexican-style foldovers with an Italian spin are brim with provolone and mozzarella cheeses as well as ripe olives and walnuts.

PER APPETIZER: 98 cal., 6 g total fat (2 g sat. fat), 9 mg chol., 217 mg sodium, 8 g carb., 1 g fiber, 5 g pro. Exchanges: 0.5 starch, 0.5 medium-fat meat, 0.5 fat. Carb choices: 0.5.

- **6 6-inch white or yellow corn tortillas**
- **4 ounces part-skim mozzarella cheese, shredded (1 cup)**
- **2 ounces provolone cheese, shredded ($^{1}/_2$ cup)**
- **$^{1}/_4$ cup chopped pitted ripe olives**
- **3 tablespoons chopped walnuts or pine nuts, toasted**
- **2 teaspoons snipped fresh oregano or $^{1}/_2$ teaspoon dried oregano, crushed**
- **1 tablespoon olive oil**
- **$^{1}/_2$ cup purchased mild salsa**
- **1 teaspoon snipped fresh oregano or $^{1}/_4$ teaspoon dried oregano, crushed**
- **Fresh oregano sprigs (optional)**

1. Preheat oven to 350°F. Stack tortillas and wrap in foil. Bake about 10 minutes or until softened. Meanwhile, in a medium bowl, combine mozzarella cheese, provolone cheese, olives, nuts, and the 2 teaspoons snipped oregano or $^{1}/_2$ teaspoon dried oregano. Spread cheese mixture onto half of each tortilla. Fold tortillas in half; secure with wooden toothpicks. Brush one side of each quesadilla with some of the oil.

2. In a large skillet or on a griddle, place quesadillas, 2 or 3 at a time, oiled sides down. Cook over medium heat about 4 minutes or until heated through, brushing with remaining oil and turning quesadillas once. Cut each quesadilla in half.

3. Meanwhile, in a small saucepan, heat salsa just until hot; stir in the 1 teaspoon snipped oregano or $^{1}/_4$ teaspoon dried oregano. If desired, garnish with oregano sprigs. Serve with quesadillas. Makes 12 appetizers.

Walnut-Olive Quesadillas

Fajita-Style Quesadillas

This recipe substitutes white corn tortillas for the more usual flour variety. If you have access to a Mexican market that sells homemade corn tortillas, use them. There's nothing better.

PER SERVING: 72 cal., 4 g total fat (2 g sat. fat), 6 mg chol., 46 mg sodium, 8 g carb., 1 g fiber, 3 g pro. Exchanges: 0.5 starch, 0.5 fat. Carb choices: 0.5.

- ½ of a medium red or green sweet pepper, seeded and cut into bite-size strips
- ½ of a medium onion, halved and thinly sliced
- 1 serrano chile pepper, halved, seeded, and cut into thin strips*
- 2 teaspoons cooking oil
- 6 4-inch or four 6-inch white corn tortillas
- Nonstick cooking spray
- ½ cup shredded Monterey Jack cheese (2 ounces)
- 1 small tomato, halved and thinly sliced
- 2 tablespoons snipped fresh cilantro
- 2 tablespoons light dairy sour cream (optional)

1. In a medium skillet, cook sweet pepper, onion, and serrano pepper in hot oil over medium-high heat for 3 to 5 minutes or until vegetables are just tender. Remove from heat.

2. Lightly coat one side of each tortilla with cooking spray. Divide cheese evenly among uncoated sides of three 4-inch or two 6-inch tortillas. Top with onion mixture, tomato slices, and cilantro. Top with remaining tortillas, coated sides up.

3. Heat a heavy skillet or griddle over medium heat. Cook quesadillas, one at a time, for 1 to 2 minutes per side or until cheese melts and tortillas are lightly browned. Cut each quesadilla into 4 wedges. Serve warm and, if desired, with sour cream. Makes 8 (2-wedge) servings.

*Test Kitchen Tip: Because chile peppers contain volatile oils that can burn your skin and eyes, avoid direct contact with them as much as possible. When working with chile peppers, wear plastic or rubber gloves. If your bare hands do touch the peppers, wash your hands and nails well with soap and water.

Fajita-Style Quesadillas

Polynesian Glazed Wings

Maryland Crab Cakes with Horseradish Sauce

This bite-sized version of an East Coast classic makes a terrific start to any party.

PER APPETIZER: 43 cal., 1 g total fat (0 g sat. fat), 19 mg chol., 178 mg sodium, 4 g carb., 0 g fiber, 5 g pro. Exchanges: 1 lean meat. Carb choices: 0.

- 1 6-ounce package frozen cooked crab, thawed, drained, and flaked
- 1/2 cup fine dry bread crumbs
- 2 tablespoons finely chopped green onion
- 2 tablespoons finely chopped green sweet pepper
- 2 tablespoons fat-free mayonnaise dressing or salad dressing
- 1 egg white
- 1/2 teaspoon dry mustard
- 1/2 teaspoon finely shredded lemon or lime peel
- 1/8 teaspoon ground black pepper
  Nonstick spray coating
- 1/4 cup plain low-fat yogurt
- 2 tablespoons fat-free mayonnaise dressing or salad dressing
- 2 tablespoons finely chopped green onion
- 1 1/2 teaspoons prepared horseradish
- 1 teaspoon finely snipped fresh parsley

1. Preheat oven to 350°F. In a medium mixing bowl, combine the crabmeat, bread crumbs, green onion, sweet pepper, mayonnaise dressing, egg white, mustard, lemon peel, and black pepper. Mix well. (If mixture seems dry, stir in 1 tablespoon milk.)

2. Gently shape mixture into 18 small patties. Lightly coat a shallow baking pan with cooking spray. Place patties in pan. Bake about 15 minutes or until the patties are a light golden brown.

3. Meanwhile, in a small bowl, stir together yogurt, mayonnaise, green onion, horseradish, and parsley. Pass with hot crab cakes. Makes 18 appetizers.

Polynesian Glazed Wings

You can make the glaze and chill it for up 48 hours. Reheat it in a small saucepan over low before using.

PER APPETIZER: 117 cal., 7 g total fat (2 g sat. fat), 47 mg chol., 90 mg sodium, 5 g carb., 0 g fiber, 8 g pro. Exchanges: 0.5 other carb., 1 medium-fat meat. Carb choices: 0.5.

- 3 pounds frozen plain chicken wing drummettes (about 30)
- 1/2 cup packed brown sugar
- 1 tablespoon cornstarch
- 2 teaspoons grated fresh ginger
- 1/4 to 1/2 teaspoon crushed red pepper
- 1/2 cup unsweetened pineapple juice
- 1/2 cup reduced-sodium chicken broth or water
- 1/4 cup finely chopped green sweet pepper
- 2 tablespoons reduced-sodium soy sauce
  Thinly sliced green onions (optional)

1. Preheat oven to 400°F. Place frozen drummettes in a 15×10×1-inch baking pan. Bake for 50 to 60 minutes or until skins are crispy.

2. Meanwhile, in a small saucepan, combine brown sugar, cornstarch, ginger, and crushed red pepper. Stir in pineapple juice, broth, sweet pepper, and soy sauce. Cook and stir over medium heat until thickened and bubbly; cook and stir for 2 minutes more. Set aside.

3. Carefully drain off any juices from baking pan. Brush chicken with some of the glaze mixture. Bake for 10 minutes more. Brush with more of the glaze mixture. Place on serving plate. If desired, sprinkle with green onions. Pass remaining glaze mixture. Makes 30 appetizers.

best-ever
holiday treats

Ricotta Cheesecake
with Apple Topper

Thank goodness the American Diabetes Association says you can have dessert if you have diabetes! What would life be without a sweet treat to end a special meal? Choose from pies, tarts, crisps, and more—all lightened and modified to fit into a diabetic meal plan.

Ricotta Cheesecake with Apple Topper

Skim ricotta cheese and reduced-fat cream cheese help make this crowd-pleasing cheesecake lighter.

PER SERVING: 212 cal., 9 g total fat (5 g sat. fat), 65 mg chol., 165 mg sodium, 26 g carb., 1 g fiber, 8 g pro. Exchanges: 1 other carb., 0.5 fruit, 1 medium-fat meat, 1 fat. Carb choices: 2.

PER SERVING WITH SUBSTITUTE: same as above, except 201 cal., 23 g carb. Carb Choices: 1.5.

Nonstick cooking spray
1   15-ounce carton light or part-skim ricotta cheese
$1^1/2$ 8-ounce packages reduced-fat cream cheese (Neufchâtel)
$^1/3$ cup sugar or sugar substitute blend* equivalent to $^1/3$ cup sugar
$^1/4$ cup honey
$^1/4$ cup unsweetened applesauce
2   tablespoons all-purpose flour
2   egg yolks
4   egg whites
1   recipe Apple Topper (see recipe, below)

1. Preheat oven to 325°F. Lightly coat a 9-inch springform pan with cooking spray; set aside.

2. In large mixing bowl, beat ricotta cheese, cream cheese, sugar, honey, applesauce, and flour with an electric mixer on medium to high speed until smooth. Add egg yolks all at once. Beat on low speed just until combined.

3. In a clean large mixing bowl, with clean beaters, beat egg whites with an electric mixer on medium to high speed until stiff peaks form. Fold one-fourth of egg whites into ricotta mixture. Fold in remaining egg whites.

4. Spoon filling into prepared pan, spreading evenly. Place in shallow baking pan. Bake 1 hour or until center appears nearly set when gently shaken.

5. Cool in pan on rack for 15 minutes. (Cheesecake will crack.) Using a thin metal spatula, loosen cheesecake from pan; cool for 30 minutes. Remove side of pan; cool completely. Cover; chill 4 hours to 24 hours. To serve, top cheesecake with Apple Topper. Makes 12 servings.

Apple Topper: Core and thinly slice 3 Jonagold or 4 McIntosh apples (about 6 cups). In a large skillet, toss apples with 1 teaspoon apple pie spice or ground cinnamon. Add $^1/4$ cup water; heat to boiling. Cover and cook over medium-high heat about 5 minutes or until apples are just tender, stirring occasionally. Drizzle with 2 tablespoons honey; toss to coat. Cool to room temperature.

*Sugar Substitutes: Choose from Splenda Sugar Blend for Baking or Equal Sugar Lite. Follow package directions to use product amount equivalent to $^1/3$ cup sugar.

Quick Tip:

Even a rich dessert can be allowed on your meal plan if you have just a few bites or a small serving. Cut a pie into 10 servings, a cheesecake into 16 servings, or a 13×9-inch cake into 20 servings. Prepare small plates of treats to send home with guests if you can't resist leftovers later.

Hazelnut-Mocha Torte

Hazelnut-Mocha Torte

For chocolate curls, draw a vegetable peeler across a side of a milk chocolate candy bar.

PER SERVING: 144 cal., 9 g total fat (1 g sat. fat), 1 mg chol., 63 mg sodium, 13 g carb., 1 g fiber, 3 g pro. Exchanges: 1 carb., 1.5 fat. Carb choices: 1.

1¹/₂ cups hazelnuts or walnuts, toasted
2   tablespoons all-purpose flour
2   teaspoons baking powder
³/₄ cup refrigerated or frozen egg product, thawed, or 3 eggs
¹/₃ cup sugar*
1   recipe White Mocha Filling (see recipe, below)
Chocolate curls (optional)

1. Preheat oven to 350°F. Grease and flour two 8×1¹/₂-inch round cake pans. Set aside. In a medium bowl, combine nuts, flour, and baking powder; set aside.

2. In a blender or food processor, combine eggs and sugar; cover and blend or process until combined. Add nut mixture. Cover and blend or process until nearly smooth, scraping side of container occasionally. Divide batter between the prepared pans; spread evenly.

3. Bake for 10 to 12 minutes or until a toothpick inserted in centers comes out clean. Cool cake layers in pans on wire racks for 10 minutes. Remove from pans. Cool completely on wire racks.

4. Place one of the cake layers on a platter. Spread top with half of the White Mocha Filling. Top with remaining cake layer and remaining filling. Loosely cover. Chill frosted cake for 2 to 24 hours. If desired, garnish with chocolate curls. Makes 16 servings.

White Mocha Filling: Place three-fourths of an 8-ounce container frozen fat-free whipped dessert topping in a medium bowl; thaw.

In a small saucepan, combine 2 ounces white baking chocolate (with cocoa butter), chopped; 1 tablespoon instant sugar-free, fat-free Suisse mocha- or French vanilla-style coffee powder; and 1 tablespoon fat-free milk. Cook and stir over low heat until melted and smooth. Remove from heat. Stir in ¹/₂ cup of the whipped topping (whipped topping will melt). Cool mixture about 5 minutes. Fold melted mixture into remaining thawed whipped topping in bowl.

*Test Kitchen Tip: We don't recommend sugar substitutes for this recipe.

Chocolate-Almond Torte

Both chocolate and cocoa powder flavor this torte, making it extra chocolaty and doubly delicious.

PER SERVING: 144 cal., 4 g total fat (2 g sat. fat), 0 mg chol., 81 mg sodium, 25 g carb., 1 g fiber, 4 g pro. Exchanges: 1.5 other carb., 0.5 fat. Carb choices: 1.5.

- 3/4 cup fat-free milk
- 1/3 cup unsweetened cocoa powder
- 2 ounces unsweetened chocolate, chopped
- 1 tablespoon balsamic vinegar
- 3 egg whites
- Nonstick cooking spray
- 3/4 cup all-purpose flour
- 2/3 cup granulated sugar*
- 1/2 teaspoon baking powder
- 1/4 teaspoon baking soda
- 1/8 teaspoon salt
- 1/4 cup granulated sugar*
- 1/4 cup sliced almonds
- 1 to 2 teaspoons powdered sugar (optional)

1. In a small saucepan, combine milk and cocoa powder. Heat over medium heat, whisking constantly, until mixture just comes to a boil. Remove from heat. Whisk in unsweetened chocolate and vinegar until smooth. Cool to room temperature. Meanwhile, in a medium mixing bowl, allow egg whites to stand at room temperature for 30 minutes.

2. Preheat oven to 350°F. Lightly coat an 8×2-inch round tart pan with removable bottom or 8-inch springform pan with cooking spray; set aside. In a large bowl, stir together flour, the 2/3 cup granulated sugar, the baking powder, baking soda, and salt. Stir cooled chocolate mixture into flour mixture until well combined (batter will be thick); set aside.

3. In a large mixing bowl, beat egg whites with an electric mixer on medium speed until soft peaks form (tips curl). Gradually add the 1/4 cup granulated sugar, about 1 tablespoon at a time, beating on high speed until stiff peaks form. Gently fold one-third of the beaten egg whites into the chocolate mixture. Fold in the remaining beaten egg whites just until combined. Spread batter in prepared baking pan. Sprinkle almonds over batter.

4. Bake 25 to 28 minutes or until a wooden toothpick inserted near the center comes out clean. Cool in pan on wire rack for 15 minutes. Remove side of pan. Cool completely. If desired, sprinkle lightly with powdered sugar before serving. Makes 12 servings.

*Test Kitchen Tip: We do not recommend sugar substitutes for this recipe.

Banana Brownie Skillet

Banana Brownie Skillet

Your own or visiting children will love this banana split disguised as a large brownie.

PER SERVING: 173 cal., 5 g total fat (3 g sat. fat), 1 mg chol., 138 mg sodium, 31 g carb., 2 g fiber, 4 g pro. Exchanges: 2 carb., 1 fat. Carb choices: 2. PER SERVING WITH SUBSTITUTE: same as above, except 151 cal., 25 g carb. Exchanges: 1.5 other carb. Carb choices: 1.5.

1 cup semisweet chocolate pieces
²/₃ cup buckwheat flour
²/₃ cup sugar or sugar substitute* blend equivalent to ²/₃ cup sugar
¹/₃ cup nonfat dry milk powder
¹/₃ cup unsweetened cocoa powder
1 teaspoon ground cinnamon
¹/₂ teaspoon baking soda
¹/₄ teaspoon salt
2 egg whites, lightly beaten
¹/₃ cup buttermilk
1 teaspoon vanilla
  Nonstick cooking spray
1 large banana, sliced
  Powdered sugar (optional)
4 cups sliced fresh strawberries (optional)
1 8-ounce container frozen light whipped dessert topping, thawed (optional)

1. In a large bowl, stir together chocolate pieces, buckwheat flour, sugar, nonfat dry milk powder, cocoa powder, cinnamon, baking soda, and salt; make a well in the center of the flour mixture.

2. In a medium bowl, stir together egg whites, buttermilk, and vanilla; add all at once to chocolate mixture. Stir until combined.

3. Lightly coat an 8- to 9-inch cast-iron skillet or a 6-inch springform pan with cooking spray. Spread batter in pan; arrange banana slices on top. Brush banana slices lightly with *lemon juice*.

4. Bake in a 350°F oven 35 to 40 minutes for the skillet or 65 to 75 minutes for the springform pan or or until a toothpick inserted in center comes out clean and edges start to pull away from the sides of the pan. For skillet, cool on wire rack 30 minutes before serving. Cool springform pan on wire rack for 10 minutes; loosen sides of pan and cool 30 minutes before removing the sides of the pan.

5. To serve, if desired, sprinkle top of brownie with powdered sugar. Or melt 1-ounce white baking chocolate and ¹/₄ teaspoon shortening in a small heavy saucepan over low heat just until melted; drizzle over brownie. Serve warm with dessert topping, if desired. Makes 12 servings (1 slice each).

***Sugar Substitutes:** Choose from Splenda Sugar Blend for Baking or Equal Sugar Lite. Follow package directions to use product amount equivalent to ²/₃ cup sugar.

Pineapple Cake with Macadamia-Apricot Topper

Need a great dessert in a hurry? Spoon the tempting topper over purchased angel food cake.

PER SERVING: 191 cal., 8 g total fat (1 g sat. fat), 39 mg chol., 91 mg sodium, 28 g carb., 1 g fiber, 4 g pro. Exchanges: 2 carb., 1.5 fat. Carb choices 2. PER SERVING WITH SUBSTITUTE: same as above, except 179 cal., 23 g carb. Exchanges: 1.5 carb. Carb choices: 1.5.

6 egg whites
3 egg yolks
1²/₃ cups cake flour
²/₃ cup sugar or sugar substitute blend* equivalent to ²/₃ cup sugar
2 teaspoons baking powder
¹/₄ teaspoon salt
¹/₂ cup unsweetened pineapple juice
¹/₄ cup canola oil
¹/₄ teaspoon cream of tartar
1 recipe Macadamia-Apricot Topper (see recipe, opposite)
2 tablespoons shredded coconut, toasted

1. Allow egg whites and yolks to stand at room temperature for 30 minutes.

2. Preheat oven to 325°F. Meanwhile, in a large bowl, stir together cake flour, sugar, baking powder, and salt. Make a well in the center of the flour mixture.

3. Add egg yolks, pineapple juice, and oil to flour mixture. Beat with an electric mixer on low speed until combined. Beat on high speed about 5 minutes or until batter is satin smooth. Thoroughly wash and dry the beaters.

4. In a very large bowl, combine egg whites and cream of tartar. Beat with electric mixer on medium speed until stiff peaks form (tips stand straight). Pour batter in a thin stream over beaten egg whites, folding gently as you pour. Pour into an ungreased 10-inch tube pan.

5. Bake for 45 to 50 minutes or until top is golden brown and springs back when lightly touched. Immediately invert cake (in the pan); cool completely. Loosen side of the cake from the pan; remove cake from pan. Place on a platter. Top with Macadamia-Apricot Topper. Sprinkle with coconut. Makes 16 servings.

Macadamia-Apricot Topper: Rinse and drain one 15-ounce can unpeeled apricot halves in light syrup. Cut apricot halves into strips; set aside. In a small saucepan, combine $2/3$ cup unsweetened pineapple juice and 2 teaspoons cornstarch. Cook and stir until thickened and bubbly; cook and stir for 2 minutes more. Stir in $1/2$ cup toasted and coarsely chopped macadamia nuts or toasted and coarsely chopped hazelnuts (see tip, page 7). Stir in apricot strips. Makes $13/4$ cups.

*Sugar Substitutes: Choose from Splenda Sugar Blend for Baking or Equal Sugar Lite. Follow package directions to use product amount equivalent to $2/3$ cup sugar.

Pineapple Cake with Macadamia-Apricot Topper

Chocolate-Orange Custards

This intensely chocolaty dessert relies on only 3 tablespoons added sugar for the whole recipe. Use a high-quality chocolate for the best flavor.

PER SERVING: 169 cal., 5 g total fat (3 g sat. fat), 3 mg chol., 122 mg sodium, 23 g carb., 1 g fiber, 8 g pro. Exchanges: 1.5 other carb., 1 very lean meat, 1 fat. Carb choices: 1.5.

Butter
Sugar
1¼ **cups fat-free milk**
3 **tablespoons sugar**
2 **ounces semisweet chocolate, coarsely chopped**
1 **vanilla bean, split lengthwise, or 1 teaspoon vanilla**
¾ **cup refrigerated or frozen egg product, thawed, or 3 eggs, lightly beaten**
½ **teaspoon orange extract**
Chocolate shavings (optional)
Kumquat slices (optional)

1. Preheat oven to 325°F. Butter bottom and 1 inch up sides of four 6-ounce oven-going star molds or custard cups. Sprinkle molds or cups lightly with sugar, shaking out excess; place in a shallow baking dish; set aside.

2. In a medium saucepan, stir together milk, the 3 tablespoons sugar, chocolate, and vanilla bean (if using). Cook and stir over medium heat until chocolate is melted. In a medium bowl, combine egg, vanilla (if using), and orange extract. If using vanilla bean, remove from milk mixture. Gradually whisk milk mixture into egg mixture. If necessary, spoon off and discard foam from surface of mixture.

3. Place baking dish on an oven rack. Pour egg mixture into molds or custard cups. Pour boiling water into the baking dish around molds or custard cups to a depth of 1 inch. Bake for 30 to 35 minutes or until a knife inserted near the centers comes out clean.

4. Remove molds or custard cups from water. Cool completely in molds or custard cups on a wire rack.

Chocolate-Orange Custards

**Mascarpone-Stuffed Figs
with Valencia Orange Glaze**

Cover and chill at least 2 hours or until ready to serve. To unmold custards, loosen edges with a knife, slipping its point in between the custard and cup to let in air. Invert a dessert plate over each custard and carefully turn mold and plate over together; remove mold from custard. If desired, garnish with chocolate shavings and kumquat slices. Makes 4 servings.

Mascarpone-Stuffed Figs with Valencia Orange Glaze

To cut the fat, stuff the figs with light cream cheese instead of rich Italian mascarpone.

PER SERVING: 133 cal., 5 g total fat (2 g sat. fat), 7 mg chol., 35 mg sodium, 22 g carb., 3 g fiber, 3 g pro. Exchanges: 1 fruit, 0.5 carb., 1 fat. Carb choices: 1.5.
PER SERVING WITH SUBSTITUTE: same as above, except 131 cal., 22 g carb.

- 3 tablespoons mascarpone cheese or reduced-fat cream cheese (Neufchâtel)
- 1 teaspoon sugar or sugar substitute* equivalent to 1 teaspoon sugar
- 8 small fresh figs**
- 3 sheets frozen phyllo dough (14×9-inch rectangles)
  Nonstick cooking spray
- 3 tablespoons very finely chopped pistachio nuts
- 1 recipe Valencia Orange Glaze (see recipe, right)

1. Preheat oven to 375°F. For filling, combine cheese, sugar, and 1 teaspoon orange peel (from the glaze at right); set aside.
2. Wash figs gently; pat dry. Cut off any stems. Quarter lengthwise, cutting almost to bottoms. If desired, remove any seeds. Using a pastry bag fitted with a large tip or a spoon, fill the fig centers with filling. Gently press each into a teardrop shape.
3. Keep phyllo covered with plastic wrap until needed. On a clean surface, coat a sheet with spray. Sprinkle with 2 teaspoons of the nuts. Repeat with phyllo, spray, and nuts to make a stack of 3 sheets.
4. Cut stack in half lengthwise, then crosswise to make 4 rectangles. Cut each rectangle in half diagonally to make 8 triangles total.
5. For each bundle, place a filled fig on its side about 1 1/2 inches from short edge of triangle. Bring up corners; fold remaining point over fig to enclose. Press edges to seal.

6. Arrange bundles on an ungreased baking sheet. Coat with spray; top with remaining nuts.
7. Bake bundles for 8 to 10 minutes or until phyllo is golden and crisp.
8. To serve, spoon warm Valencia Orange Glaze onto dessert plates. Top with phyllo-wrapped figs and orange wedges. Serve warm. Makes 8 servings.

Valencia Orange Glaze: Cut 2 Valencia or navel oranges into 8 wedges each; set aside. From 2 other oranges, finely shred enough peel to produce 1 1/2 teaspoons peel (use 1 teaspoon in the mascarpone filling). Juice the 2 oranges; measure and add enough orange juice to equal 1 cup juice total.

In a large skillet, heat 1 teaspoon olive oil over medium heat. Add orange wedges; cook about 3 minutes or until brown, turning to brown evenly. Remove wedges; set aside.

In a small saucepan, stir together orange juice, 1 tablespoon honey, 2 teaspoons arrowroot or cornstarch, and remaining 1/2 teaspoon orange peel. Cook and stir until thickened (do not boil if using arrowroot). (If using cornstarch, cook and stir until thickened and bubbly. Cook and stir for 2 minutes more.) Remove saucepan from heat. Serve with figs. Makes 1 cup glaze.

***Sugar Substitutes:** Choose from Splenda granular or Sweet'N Low bulk or packets. Follow the package directions to use product amount equivalent to 1 teaspoon sugar.

****Test Kitchen Tip:** If you can't find fresh figs, use 8 dried figs. In medium saucepan, combine dried figs and enough water to cover. Heat to boiling; reduce heat. Cover and simmer for 5 minutes. Remove from heat; let stand for 15 minutes. Drain and cool. Continue cutting and filling as directed in Step 2.

Nutty Cheese-Topped Figs
These little bites make a classy finale or buffet choice.

PER SERVING: 30 cal., 2 g total fat (1 g sat. fat), 2 mg chol., 15 mg sodium, 3 g carb., 1 g fiber, 1 g pro. Exchanges: 0.5 fat. Carb choices: 0.

10   dried **Calimyrna (light) figs**
1/4   cup **light tub-style cream cheese**
1 1/2   teaspoons **finely shredded lemon peel**
10   **Brazil nuts or toasted whole almonds (see tip, page 7), or 20 hazelnuts**
2   teaspoons **honey (optional)**

1. Trim off fig stems. Cut figs in half horizontally.
2. Spoon cream cheese into a small resealable plastic bag. Snip off a corner. Pipe a little cream cheese onto each fig half. Sprinkle with lemon peel.
3. Cut large nuts in half. Place a nut on each fig half. If desired, top with honey. Makes 20 servings.

Chocolate Chip Pumpkin Bars

These treats feature an array of healthful ingredients: whole wheat flour, pumpkin, nuts, and chocolate.

PER BAR: 90 cal., 4 g total fat (1 g sat. fat), 0 mg chol., 77 mg sodium, 12 g carb., 1 g fiber, 2 g pro. Exchanges: 1 other carb., 0.5 fat. Carb Choices: 1.

Nonstick cooking spray
- 1   cup all-purpose flour
- 1   cup whole wheat flour
- $^3/_4$ cup granulated sugar
- $^1/_2$ cup pecans or walnuts, finely chopped (optional)
- 2   teaspoons baking powder
- 1   teaspoon ground cinnamon
- $^1/_2$ teaspoon baking soda
- $^1/_2$ teaspoon salt
- 1   cup refrigerated or frozen egg product, thawed, or 4 eggs, lightly beaten
- 1   15-ounce can pumpkin
- $^1/_2$ cup cooking oil
- $^1/_4$ cup fat-free milk
- $^1/_3$ cup miniature semisweet chocolate pieces
- 2   tablespoons miniature semisweet chocolate pieces
- $1^1/_2$ to 2 teaspoons powdered sugar (optional)

1. Preheat oven to 350°F. Lightly coat a 15×10×1-inch baking pan with cooking spray; set aside. In a large bowl, stir together all-purpose flour, whole wheat flour, granulated sugar, nuts (if using), baking powder, cinnamon, baking soda, and salt.

2. In a medium bowl, combine egg, pumpkin, oil, and milk. Add pumpkin mixture to flour mixture along with $^1/_3$ cup chocolate pieces; stir just until combined. Spread batter evenly in prepared pan. Sprinkle top with 2 tablespoons chocolate pieces. Bake about 25 minutes or until a toothpick inserted in the center comes out clean. Cool on a wire rack. If desired, sprinkle lightly with powdered sugar. Cut into bars. Makes 36 bars.

Chocolate Chip Pumpkin Bars

Nuts-About-Cranberries Tart

Sweet-tart fruit contrasts nicely with slightly salted pistachios and buttery almonds.

PER SERVING: 165 cal., 9 g total fat (4 g sat. fat), 15 mg chol., 62 mg sodium, 20 g carb., 2 g fiber, 3 g pro. Exchanges: 1 carb., 2 fat. Carb choices: 1.

- **1 recipe Rich Pastry (see recipe, opposite)**
- **¼ cup packed brown sugar***
- **2 tablespoons butter**
- **1 cup fresh cranberries**
- **1 medium pear, cored and chopped**
- **⅓ cup lightly salted pistachio nuts**
- **⅓ cup sliced almonds**
- **½ teaspoon vanilla**

1. Preheat oven to 450°F. On a lightly floured surface, use your hands to slightly flatten the Rich Pastry dough. Roll dough from center to edges into a 15×6-inch rectangle. Transfer dough to an ungreased 13¾×4-inch tart pan with a removable bottom. Ease pastry into tart pan, being careful not to stretch pastry. (Or roll dough from center to edge into a 10-inch circle. Wrap pastry around rolling pin. Unroll into an ungreased 9-inch tart pan with a removable bottom.) Press pastry into the fluted sides of the tart pan. Trim pastry even with edges of pan.

2. Line pastry with a double thickness of foil. Bake for 8 minutes. Remove foil. Bake for 3 to 4 minutes more or until set and dry. Cool crust in pan on a wire rack. Reduce oven temperature to 375°F.

3. In a medium saucepan, combine brown sugar and butter. Cook and stir over medium heat until brown sugar is melted.

4. Add cranberries and pear; cook and stir until bubbly. Remove from heat. Stir in pistachio nuts, almonds, and vanilla. Spoon filling into crust, spreading evenly. Place tart pan on a baking sheet.

5. Bake for 20 to 25 minutes or until juices are bubbly around edges and pastry is golden brown. Cool in pan on wire rack. Remove sides of pan. Using wide spatulas, remove tart from bottom of pan; transfer to a platter. Makes 12 servings.

Rich Pastry: In a medium bowl, combine 1 cup all-purpose flour, 1/4 cup whole wheat pastry flour or whole wheat flour, and 1 tablespoon granulated sugar.* Using a pastry blender, cut in 1/4 cup butter until pieces are pea size. In a small bowl, combine 2 tablespoons refrigerated or frozen egg product, thawed, and 2 tablespoons ice water. Gradually stir water mixture into flour mixture until moistened. (If necessary, stir additional cold water, 1 teaspoon at a time, into mixture to moisten.) Shape dough into a ball.

*Test Kitchen Tip: We don't recommend sugar substitutes for this recipe.

Fruit Cups with Ginger Nuts

Use leftover nuts to jazz up salads and desserts.

PER SERVING: 123 cal., 5 g total fat (1 g sat. fat), 0 mg chol., 10 mg sodium, 21 g carb., 3 g fiber, 2 g pro. Exchanges: 1 fruit, 0.5 carb., 0.5 fat. Carb choices: 1.5.
PER SERVING WITH SUBSTITUTES: same as above, except 118 cal., 20 g carb. Carb choices: 1.

- **1/3 cup mango nectar or orange juice**
- **1 teaspoon cornstarch**
- **1/4 teaspoon ground ginger**
- **1 small banana, sliced**
- **2 small oranges, peeled and sectioned**
- **1/4 cup Ginger Nuts (see recipe, below)**
  Frozen light whipped dessert topping, thawed (optional)

1. In a small saucepan, combine mango nectar, cornstarch, and ginger. Cook and stir until thickened and bubbly; cook and stir for 2 minutes more. Remove from heat. Gently stir in banana; cool.

2. Divide banana mixture and orange sections among 4 dessert dishes. Top with Ginger Nuts and, if desired, whipped topping. Serve immediately. Makes 4 servings.

Ginger Nuts: Preheat oven to 350°F. In a 13×9×2-inch baking pan, combine 1/2 cup macadamia nuts, 1/2 cup whole almonds, 1/2 cup lightly salted pistachio nuts, and 1/2 cup coarsely chopped pecans. Bake 10 minutes. Cool on a wire rack. Reduce oven temperature to 325°F.

Meanwhile, in a large bowl, combine 1 egg white and 1 teaspoon water; beat with a wire whisk or rotary beater until frothy. Discard half of the egg white mixture. To the remaining egg white mixture, stir in 2 tablespoons granulated sugar or sugar substitute* equivalent to 2 tablespoons granulated sugar, 2 tablespoons packed brown sugar or brown sugar substitute* equivalent to 2 tablespoons brown sugar, and 3/4 teaspoon ground ginger. Stir in cooled nuts.

Lightly coat the same baking pan with cooking spray. Spread nuts in a single layer in prepared pan. Bake for 15 to 20 minutes or until nuts appear dry, stirring once halfway through baking. Spread nut mixture on a piece of foil coated with cooking spray, separating into individual pieces or small clusters; cool. Store in a tightly covered container in the refrigerator for up to 1 week. Makes about 2 1/4 cups.

*Sugar Substitutes: For the granulated sugar, choose from Splenda granular or Sweet'N Low bulk or packets. For the brown sugar, choose from Sweet'N Low Brown or Sugar Twin Granulated Brown. Follow package directions to use product amounts equivalent to 2 tablespoons of each sugar.

Fruit Cups with Ginger Nuts

Plum Clafouti Tarts

Plum Clafouti Tarts

Although cherries are the traditional fruit for clafouti,
this updated tart version uses plums.

PER SERVING: 162 cal., 3 g total fat (2 g sat. fat), 9 mg chol., 138 mg sodium,
28 g carb., 1 g fiber, 5 g pro. Exchanges: 2 other carb., 0.5 fat. Carb
choices: 2.

PER SERVING WITH SUBSTITUTE: same as above, except 130 cal.,
20 g carb, Exchanges: 1.5 other carb. Carb Choices: 1.

    Nonstick cooking spray
4   sheets frozen phyllo dough (14×9-inch rectangles),
    thawed
$^1/_3$ cup refrigerated or frozen egg product, thawed, or
    1 egg and 1 egg white, lightly beaten
3   tablespoons granulated sugar or sugar substitute*
    equivalent to 3 tablespoons sugar
1   tablespoon fat-free milk
$^1/_4$ teaspoon vanilla
    Dash salt

$^1/_2$ cup light dairy sour cream
$^1/_3$ cup all-purpose flour
2   small ripe plums, halved and pitted
1   teaspoon sifted powdered sugar (optional)

1. Preheat oven to 375°F. Lightly coat four 6-ounce
custard cups or ramekins with cooking spray; set aside.
Unfold phyllo dough; keep covered with plastic wrap,
removing sheets as you need them. Lay one sheet of
phyllo dough on a flat surface; lightly coat with cooking
spray. Top with a second phyllo sheet; lightly coat with
cooking spray. Using a sharp knife or pizza cutter, cut
phyllo stack lengthwise into two 14-inch-long strips. Cut
each strip crosswise into two rectangles, making four
rectangles. Repeat with the remaining phyllo sheets and
cooking spray to make four more rectangles.

2. Gently press one phyllo rectangle into one of the
prepared custard cups, pressing dough into the side of
the cup. Place another phyllo rectangle crosswise over

the first rectangle, pressing it into the side of the custard cup. Repeat with remaining phyllo rectangles and custard cups. Set aside.

3. In a medium bowl, whisk together eggs, granulated sugar, milk, vanilla, and salt. Whisk in the sour cream until mixture is smooth. Add flour, whisking until mixture is smooth.

4. Divide batter among phyllo-lined custard cups. Place a plum half, cut side up, in the center of each custard cup.

5. Bake 20 to 25 minutes or until mixture is puffed, just starting to brown, and the batter around the plum is set. Cool on wire rack about 15 minutes before serving. If desired, sprinkle with powdered sugar; serve warm. Makes 4 servings.

*Sugar Substitutes: Choose from Splenda granular or Sweet'N Low bulk or packets. Follow package directions to use product amount equivalent to 3 tablespoons sugar. Decrease baking time to 18 to 22 minutes.

1. Preheat oven to 375°F. For topping, in a bowl, stir together $^{1}/_{2}$ cup flour, $^{1}/_{4}$ cup sugar, and the oats. Using a pastry blender, cut in vegetable oil spread until the mixture resembles coarse crumbs. Stir in pine nuts.

2. For filling, in a large bowl, stir together $^{1}/_{4}$ cup sugar, the 2 tablespoons flour, and the nutmeg. Add pear slices, cherries, and almond extract. Toss gently to coat. Transfer filling to an ungreased 2-quart rectangular or square baking dish. Sprinkle topping over filling.

3. Bake for 30 to 35 minutes or until filling is bubbly and topping is lightly browned. Cool in dish on wire rack about 20 minutes. Serve crisp warm. Makes 10 (about $^{1}/_{3}$-cup) servings.

*Sugar Substitutes: Choose Splenda granular or Sweet'N Low bulk or packets. Follow package directions to use product amount equivalent to $^{1}/_{4}$ cup sugar.

Pear-Cherry Crisp
with Pine Nut Topper

Pear-Cherry Crisp with Pine Nut Topper

With a choice between pears or peaches,
you can serve this dessert any time of year.

PER SERVING: 180 cal., 6 g total fat (1 g sat. fat), 0 mg chol., 38 mg sodium, 29 g carb., 3 g fiber, 3 g pro. Exchanges: 1.5 other carb., 0.5 fruit, 1 fat. Carb choices: 2.
PER SERVING WITH SUBSTITUTE: same as above, except 146 cal., 21 g carb. Exchange: 1 other carb. Carb choices: 1.5

$^{1}/_{2}$ cup white whole wheat flour or all-purpose flour
$^{1}/_{4}$ cup sugar or sugar substitute* equivalent to
    $^{1}/_{4}$ cup sugar
3 tablespoons rolled oats
$^{1}/_{3}$ cup tub-style 50 to 70% vegetable oil spread, chilled
$^{1}/_{4}$ cup pine nuts
$^{1}/_{4}$ cup sugar or sugar substitute* equivalent to
    $^{1}/_{4}$ cup sugar
2 tablespoons white whole wheat flour or
    all-purpose flour
$^{1}/_{4}$ teaspoon ground nutmeg
4 cups sliced, cored fresh pears or pitted fresh peaches
1 cup fresh or frozen unsweetened pitted dark
    sweet cherries
$^{1}/_{2}$ teaspoon almond extract

Peachy Raspberry Cobblers

Sweet peaches and tart raspberries pair up
for these individual cobblers.

PER SERVING: 160 cal., 4 g total fat (2 g sat. fat), 35 mg chol., 120 mg
sodium, 28 g carb., 4 g fiber, 4 g pro. Exchanges: 1 starch, 0.5 other
carb., 0.5 fruit, 0.5 fat.

  1 **cup all-purpose flour**
1¹/₂ **teaspoons baking powder**
¹/₄ **teaspoon ground ginger or ground cinnamon**
¹/₈ **teaspoon salt**
  2 **tablespoons butter or margarine**
¹/₄ **cup sugar**
  4 **teaspoons cornstarch**
¹/₃ **cup water**
  3 **cups fresh or frozen unsweetened peach slices**
  2 **cups fresh or frozen unsweetened raspberries**
¹/₃ **cup plain fat-free yogurt**
  1 **slightly beaten egg**
    Ground ginger or ground cinnamon (optional)

1. For topping, in a medium bowl, stir together flour, baking powder, ¹/₄ teaspoon ginger, and salt. Using a pastry blender, cut in butter until mixture resembles coarse crumbs. Set aside.

2. For filling, in a large saucepan, stir together sugar and cornstarch. Stir in water. Add peach slices and raspberries. Cook and stir until thickened and bubbly. Keep filling hot while finishing topping.

3. Preheat oven to 400°F. In a small bowl, stir together yogurt and egg. Add yogurt mixture to flour mixture, stirring just until moistened.

4. Divide filling among eight 6-ounce custard cups or four 10- to 12-ounce casseroles.* Drop the topping from a spoon onto hot filling. Drop 1 mound into each custard cup or 2 mounds into each casserole. Place custard cups or casseroles on a baking sheet.

5. Bake for 15 to 20 minutes or until a wooden toothpick inserted into topping comes out clean. Cool slightly. If desired, sprinkle with additional ginger. Serve warm. Makes 8 servings.

***Test Kitchen Tip:** To make a large cobbler, transfer hot filling to a 2-quart square baking dish. Drop topping from a spoon into 8 mounds on top of hot filling. Bake in a 400°F oven about 20 minutes or until a wooden toothpick inserted into topping comes out clean.

Caramel Apple Crisp

Offer your guests a topper of low-fat ice cream
or frozen yogurt. If you have room in your day's meal plan,
indulge yourself, too.

PER SERVING: 172 cal., 4 g total fat (1 g sat. fat), 0 mg chol., 76 mg sodium,
34 g carb., 3 g fiber, 2 g pro. Exchanges: 1 other carb., 1 fruit, 1 fat. Carb
choices: 2.

  1 **pound small cooking apples, cut into ¹/₂-inch slices (about 5 cups)**
¹/₄ **cup low-calorie cranberry juice or water**
  1 **teaspoon finely shredded lemon peel**
¹/₄ **teaspoon ground allspice**
  1 **cup low-fat granola**
¹/₄ **cup chopped pecans, toasted (see tip, page 7)**
¹/₄ **cup fat-free caramel ice cream topping**
    Light or low-fat vanilla ice cream or frozen yogurt (optional)

1. In 10-inch skillet, combine apple slices, cranberry juice, and lemon peel. Cook, stirring occasionally, over medium-high heat for 6 to 8 minutes or until apples are crisp-tender. Remove from heat. Sprinkle allspice over apples.

2. Spoon apple mixture into 6 dessert dishes. Sprinkle each serving with granola and nuts. Drizzle with caramel topping. If desired, serve with ice cream. Makes 6 (¹/₄-cup) servings.

Peachy Raspberry Cobblers

Peach Crumble Tart

This fruit tart has peaches and a crumbly oatmeal topper that's seasoned with cinnamon.

PER SERVING: 177 cal., 7 g total fat (2 g sat. fat), 5 mg chol., 65 mg sodium, 27 g carb., 2 g fiber, 3 g pro. Exchanges: 1 other carb., 1 fruit, 1.5 fat. Carb choices: 2

1	recipe **Oil Pastry** (see recipe, opposite)
1/2	cup regular rolled oats
1/4	cup all-purpose flour
2	tablespoons packed brown sugar
1 1/2	teaspoon ground cinnamon
2	tablespoons butter or margarine, melted
1/4	cup granulated sugar
1	tablespoon all-purpose flour

6 medium peaches (2 pounds), peeled and thinly sliced (about 6 cups), or two 16-ounce package frozen unsweetened peach slices, thawed and undrained (about 7 cups)
  Frozen light whipped dessert topping, thawed (optional)

1. Preheat oven to 450°F. Prepare Oil Pastry. On a lightly floured surface, slightly flatten dough. Roll dough from center to edges into a 12-inch circle. Transfer pastry to a 10-inch tart pan with a removable bottom (be careful as pastry will be very tender). Press pastry into fluted side of tart pan. Trim pastry to edge of pan; do not prick. Line with double thickness of foil. Bake for 8 minutes. Remove foil. Bake for 5 to 6 minutes more or until golden.

Peach Crumble Tart

Cool on a wire rack. Reduce oven temperature to 375°F.

2. Meanwhile, for topping, in small bowl, combine oats, the ¹/₄ cup flour, brown sugar, and ¹/₂ teaspoon cinnamon. Stir in melted butter. Set aside.

3. For filling, in large bowl, stir together granulated sugar, 1 tablespoon flour, and remaining 1 teaspoon cinnamon. Add peaches; toss gently to coat.

4. Spread filling evenly into tart shell. Sprinkle with topping. Bake about 50 minutes or until edge is bubbly and topping is browned. Serve warm or cool. If desired, top with additional peaches and whipped topping. Makes 12 servings.

Oil Pastry: In a medium bowl, combine 1¹/₃ cups all-purpose flour and ¹/₄ teaspoon salt. Using a fork, stir ¹/₄ cup cooking oil and 3 tablespoons fat-free milk into flour mixture. If necessary, stir in an additional tablespoon milk to moisten (dough will appear crumbly). Form dough into a ball.

Strawberry
Bavarian Pie

Strawberry Bavarian Pie

Naturally low-fat ladyfinger sponge cakes form the crust for this light, strawberry-flavored pie. Shop for soft ladyfingers at bakeries or grocery stores; the crispy ones will not work as well.

PER SERVING: 97 cal., 2 g total fat (2 g sat. fat), 31 mg chol., 31 mg sodium, 16 g carb., 1 g fiber, 3 g pro. Exchanges: 1 other carb., 0.5 fat. Carb choices: 1.

- 3 **cups fresh strawberries**
- ¹/₄ **cup sugar**
- 1 **envelope unflavored gelatin**
- 3 **slightly beaten egg whites**
- 1 **3-ounce package ladyfingers, split**
- 2 **tablespoons orange juice**
- ¹/₂ **of an 8-ounce container frozen light whipped dessert topping, thawed (about 1 ²/₃ cups)**
  Frozen light whipped dessert topping, thawed (optional)
  Strawberry fans (optional)

1. Place the 3 cups strawberries in a blender or food processor. Cover; blend or process until smooth. Measure the strawberries (you should have about 1³/₄ cups).

2. In a medium saucepan, combine the sugar and gelatin. Stir in the blended strawberries. Cook and stir over medium heat until the mixture bubbles and the gelatin is dissolved.

3. Gradually stir about half of the gelatin mixture into the slightly beaten egg whites. Return all of the mixture to the saucepan. Cook, stirring constantly, over low heat for 2 to 3 minutes or until slightly thickened. Do not boil. Pour mixture into a bowl. Chill just until the mixture mounds slightly when dropped from a spoon, stirring occasionally.

4. Meanwhile, cut about half of the split ladyfingers in half crosswise; stand these on end around the outside edge of a 9- or 9¹/₂-inch tart pan with removable bottom or a 9-inch springform pan. Arrange the remaining split ladyfingers in bottom of pan. Slowly drizzle the orange juice over the ladyfingers.

5. Fold whipped topping into strawberry mixture; spoon into the ladyfinger-lined pan. Cover and chill for at least 2 hours or until set. If desired, garnish with additional whipped topping and strawberry fans. Makes 10 servings.

Gingered Shortcake Bites

Look for crystallized ginger in your
supermarket's produce or spice section.

PER SERVING: 83 cal., 2 g total fat (1 g sat. fat), 6 mg chol., 65 mg sodium,
14 g carb., 1 g fiber, 2 g pro. Exchanges: 0.5 starch, 0.5 other carb.,
0.5 fat. Carb choices: 1.
PER SERVING WITH SUBSTITUTE: same as above, except 75 cal.,
11 g carb.

Nonstick cooking spray
1 cup all-purpose flour
2 tablespoons packed brown sugar or brown sugar
substitute* equivalent to 2 tablespoons brown sugar
1 1/2 teaspoons finely snipped crystallized ginger or
1/2 teaspoon ground ginger
1 teaspoon baking powder
1/8 teaspoon baking soda
2 tablespoons butter
1/2 cup buttermilk
3/4 cup frozen fat-free whipped dessert topping, thawed
1/4 cup fat-free dairy sour cream
1/4 teaspoon ground ginger
1 cup fresh chopped strawberries and/or small
blueberries
Finely snipped crystallized ginger (optional)

1. Preheat oven to 450°F. Lightly coat a baking sheet
with cooking spray; set aside. In a medium bowl, combine
flour, brown sugar, the 1 1/2 teaspoons crystallized ginger
or 1/2 teaspoon ground ginger, baking powder, and
baking soda. Using a pastry blender, cut in butter until
mixture resembles coarse crumbs. Make a well in the
center of flour mixture. Add buttermilk all at once. Using
a fork, stir just until moistened.
2. Drop dough by slightly rounded tablespoons into
12 mounds on the prepared baking sheet. Bake for 8 to
10 minutes or until lightly golden and a toothpick inserted
into centers comes out clean. Cool on a wire rack.
3. In a bowl, combine whipped topping, sour cream,
and the 1/4 teaspoon ground ginger. Set aside 1/3 cup of
the mixture. Fold berries into remaining mixture.
4. Split shortcakes in half horizontally. Spoon berry
mixture on shortcake bottoms. Add tops; spoon reserved
topping mixture on top. If desired, garnish with snipped
crystallized ginger. Makes 12 servings.
*Sugar Substitutes: Choose from Sweet'N Low Brown or
Sugar Twin Granulated Brown. Follow package
directions to use product amount equivalent to 2
tablespoons brown sugar.

Black Forest Tartlets

Tiny chocolate crusts hold a chocolate pudding that is
studded and crowned with cherries.

PER SERVING: 194 cal., 9 g total fat (3 g sat. fat), 11 mg chol., 197 mg
sodium, 22 g carb., 1 g fiber, 5 g pro. Exchanges: 1.5 other carb., 1.5 fat.
Carb choices: 1.5.
PER SERVING WITH SUBSTITUTE: same as above, except 181 cal.,
19 g carb. Exchanges: 1 other carb. Carb choices: 1.

1/3 cup tub-style 60 to 70% vegetable oil spread
1/2 of an 8-ounce package reduced-fat cream cheese
(Neufchâtel), softened
2 tablespoons packed brown sugar or brown sugar
substitute* equivalent to 2 tablespoons brown sugar
2 tablespoons unsweetened cocoa powder
1 cup all-purpose flour
1 4-serving-size package sugar-free, fat-free instant
chocolate pudding mix
1 3/4 cups fat-free milk
1/2 teaspoon almond extract
2 tablespoons snipped dried tart cherries
24 frozen unsweetened tart red cherries,
thawed and drained

1. Preheat oven to 350°F. For pastry, in a mixing bowl,
beat vegetable oil spread, cream cheese, brown sugar,
and cocoa powder until combined. Stir in the flour. Press
a rounded teaspoon of pastry evenly into the bottom and
up the sides of 24 ungreased 1 3/4-inch muffin cups.
2. Bake for 15 minutes or until pastry is dry, evenly
colored, and set. Cool pastry in cups on a wire rack for
5 minutes. Carefully transfer pastry cups to a wire rack
to cool completely.
3. Meanwhile, in a medium bowl, combine pudding
mix, milk, and almond extract. Whisk for 1 minute.
Cover; chill 5 minutes or until mixture sets up slightly.
Transfer half of the pudding mixture to an airtight
container; chill for another use. Fold dried cherries into
remaining mixture.
4. Generously spoon or pipe remaining pudding
mixture into cooled pastry cups. To serve, top each
tartlet with a tart cherry. Makes 8 (3-tart) servings.
*Sugar Substitutes: Choose from Sweet'N Low Brown or
Sugar Twin Granulated Brown. Follow package
directions to use product amount equivalent to
2 tablespoons brown sugar.

(party on)

Keep your stress low during the holidays with these useful party-planning tips:

1. **Start early.** Send a "save the date" card a few weeks in advance, then send invitations shortly after.
2. **Pick a less-than-prime time.** During the holiday season, people are more likely to make it to your party if you have it on a weeknight or a Sunday afternoon or evening.
3. **Keep it (fairly) short and sweet**—three hours is a nice time frame. Or guests can stop by for an open house.
4. **Pick a theme and a color scheme**—then keep your eye out for elements that fit both. As you prepare for the party, you might find a vase here, a scrap of ribbon there.
4. **Vary the guest list.** Try to put people together who don't know each other. A mix of young and old lends to the diversity of the list.
5. **Serve simple food.** Serve finger foods for quick and easy munching. No time to bake? Buy specialty cookies at the bakery and ask about availability of diabetes-friendly types.
6. **Serve a little holiday cheer,** from a festive and bubbly drink to a comforting, warm punch. Alcohol is optional, of course.

Black Forest Tartlets

Walnut-Apricot Thumbprints

Be sure to use low-sugar preserves for the filling.

PER COOKIE: 60 cal., 3 g total fat (1 g sat. fat), 3 mg chol., 22 mg sodium, 7 g carb., 1 g fiber, 1 g pro. Exchanges: 0.5 carb., 0.5 fat. Carb choices: 0.5.

PER COOKIE WITH SUBSTITUTES: same as above, except 55 cal., 6 g carb.

1/4 **cup butter, softened**
1/4 **cup granulated sugar or sugar substitute blend* equivalent to** 1/4 **cup granulated sugar**
1/4 **cup packed brown sugar or brown sugar substitute blend* equivalent to** 1/4 **cup brown sugar**
1/2 **teaspoon baking powder**
1/4 **teaspoon ground cinnamon or ground cardamom**
1/8 **teaspoon baking soda**
2 **egg whites**
1/2 **teaspoon vanilla**
1/2 **cup all-purpose flour**
1/4 **cup whole wheat pastry flour or whole wheat flour**
1 **cup quick-cooking rolled oats**
1 **egg white, lightly beaten**
3/4 **cup finely chopped walnuts and/or pecans**
1/4 **cup low-sugar apricot, red raspberry, and/or strawberry preserves**

1. In a large bowl, beat butter with an electric mixer on medium to high speed for 30 seconds. Add granulated sugar, brown sugar, baking powder, cinnamon, and baking soda. Beat until combined, scraping side of bowl occasionally.

2. Beat in the 2 egg whites and the vanilla until combined. Beat in as much of the all-purpose flour and whole wheat flour as you can with the mixer. Using a wooden spoon, stir in any remaining flour and the oats. Cover and chill the dough about 2 hours or until easy to handle.

3. Preheat oven to 375°F. Lightly grease 2 large cookie sheets or line with parchment paper. Shape dough into $^3/_4$-inch balls. Roll in the egg white; roll in nuts to coat. Place on prepared cookie sheets. Using your thumb, make an indentation in the center of each cookie.

4. Bake for 7 to 8 minutes or until edges are golden brown. If indentations puff during baking, gently press the back of a measuring teaspoon into indentations when cookies are removed from oven. Cool cookies on cookie sheet for 1 minute. Transfer to a wire rack; cool.

5. Just before serving, spoon preserves into indentations in cookies. Makes about 36 cookies.

*Sugar Substitutes: For the granulated sugar, choose from Splenda Sugar Blend for Baking or Equal Sugar Lite. For the brown sugar, choose Splenda Brown Sugar Blend. Follow package directions to use product amounts equivalent to $^1/_4$ cup of each sugar.

Make-Ahead Directions: Layer unfilled cookies between waxed paper in an airtight container. Cover; seal. Store at room temperature for up to 2 days or freeze for up to 3 months. To serve, thaw cookies, if frozen. Just before serving, spoon preserves into indentations in cookies.

Shortbread "Flatbreads" with Ruby Chutney

With only 131 calories, two of these crispy shortbread triangles capped with the four-fruit chutney are a terrific way to end any meal.

PER SERVING: 131 cal., 7 g total fat (3 g sat. fat), 8 mg chol., 54 mg sodium, 17 g carb., 1 g fiber, 1 g pro. Exchanges: 1 other carb., 1 fat. Carb choices: 1.

- **1 cup all-purpose flour**
- **$^1/_4$ cup white whole wheat flour or whole wheat flour**
- **3 tablespoons granulated sugar***
- **$^1/_4$ cup chilled butter, cut up**
- **$^1/_4$ cup chilled tub-style 60 to 70% vegetable oil spread**
- **$^3/_4$ cup fresh cranberries**
- **$^1/_4$ cup dried tart cherries**
- **3 tablespoons packed brown sugar***
- **2 tablespoons red wine vinegar or balsamic vinegar**

Shortbread "Flatbreads" with Ruby Chutney

- **2 tablespoons pomegranate juice or cranberry juice**
- **$^1/_2$ cup fresh or frozen unsweetened red raspberries**
- **$^1/_4$ cup finely chopped pecans, toasted (see tip, page 7)**

1. Preheat oven to 375°F. For shortbreads: In a large bowl, stir together all-purpose flour, whole wheat flour, and granulated sugar. Using a pastry blender, cut in butter and vegetable oil spread until mixture resembles fine crumbs and starts to cling. Using your hands, shape the mixture into a ball and knead just until smooth.

2. Between two pieces of waxed paper, roll dough to a 15×9-inch rectangle about $^1/_8$ inch thick. Using a pastry wheel or pizza cutter, cut dough into fifteen 3-inch squares. Cut each square diagonally in half to make triangles (30 triangles total). Using a large spatula, carefully transfer triangles to ungreased baking sheets. If dough tears when transferring to the baking sheets, use your fingertips to gently press the dough back together.

3. Bake about 8 minutes or just until edges start to brown. Transfer to a wire rack; let cool.

4. Meanwhile, for chutney: In a small saucepan, combine cranberries, cherries, brown sugar, vinegar, and pomegranate juice. Bring to boiling, stirring constantly; reduce heat. Simmer, uncovered, about 5 minutes or until mixture is thickened and liquid is syrupy. Stir in raspberries; remove from heat. Cool chutney to room temperature.

5. Serve chutney on top of shortbreads and sprinkle with pecans. Makes 15 servings (2 flatbreads and about 1 tablespoon chutney per serving).

*Sugar Substitutes: We do not recommend sugar substitutes for this recipe.

Make-Ahead Directions: Prepare as directed above. Place cooled flatbreads in an airtight container. Cover; seal. Store at room temperature for up to 3 days or freeze for up to 1 month. If frozen, thaw at room temperature before serving. Cover chutney and store in the refrigerator for up to 1 week.

Gingerbread Cookies

Switching to a low-fat spread for half the butter cuts the saturated fat.

PER 3-INCH COOKIE: 73 cal., 2 g total fat (1 g sat. fat), 3 mg chol., 73 mg sodium, 12 g carb., 0 g fiber, 1 g pro. Exchanges: 1 carb. Carb choices: 1.

- ¼ cup butter, softened
- ¼ cup 50 to 70 percent vegetable oil spread
- ½ cup packed brown sugar*
- 2 teaspoons ground ginger
- 1 teaspoon baking soda
- 1 teaspoon ground cinnamon
- ¼ teaspoon salt
- ¼ teaspoon ground cloves
- ¼ cup full-flavor molasses
- ¼ cup refrigerated or frozen egg product, thawed, or 1 egg
- 2 cups all-purpose flour
- ¾ cup white whole wheat flour or whole wheat flour
  Nonstick cooking sprayr
- 1 recipe Cream Cheese Frosting (optional) (see recipe, below)

1. In a large bowl, combine butter and spread; beat with an electric mixer on high speed for 30 seconds. Add brown sugar, ginger, baking soda, cinnamon, salt, and cloves. Beat until mixed, scraping side of bowl. Beat in molasses and egg. (Mixture will look curdled.) Add flours, beating just until combined. Divide in half. Cover and chill for 2 to 3 hours or until easy to handle.

2. Preheat oven to 375°F. Coat cookie sheets with spray; set aside. On a lightly floured surface, roll dough, half at a time, to ⅛-inch thickness. Using a 2- to 3-inch cookie cutter, cut out shapes, rerolling scraps. Arrange 1 inch apart on prepared cookie sheets.

3. Bake for 4 to 6 minutes or until firm. Cool on sheets on wire racks for 1 minute. Transfer to racks; cool. If desired, frost with Cream Cheese Frosing. Makes 36 (3-inch) cookies.

*Test Kitchen Tip: We don't recommend sugar substitutes in this recipe.

Gingerbread Cookies with Cream Cheese Frosting

Cream Cheese Frosting

If you like, thin this frosting with fat-free milk to make it a drizzling consistency and add food coloring for tints.

PER TEASPOON: 28 cal., 0 g total fat (0 g sat. fat), 1 mg chol., 8 mg sodium, 6 g carb., 0 g fiber, 0 g pro. Exchanges: 0.5 carb. Carb choices: 0.5.

- ½ of an 8-ounce package reduced-fat cream cheese (Neufchâtel), softened
- 1 teaspoon vanilla
- ½ teaspoon butter flavoring (optional)
- 3 to 3½ cups powdered sugar*
  Food coloring (optional)

1. In a large mixing bowl, beat cream cheese, vanilla, and butter flavoring (if using) with electric mixer on medium speed until very smooth.

2. Gradually beat in enough powdered sugar to make a frosting of spreading or piping consistency. If desired, tint frosting with food coloring. Makes about 1¼ cups (sixty 1-teaspoon servings).

Peanut-Apple Crunch Balls

Wetting your hands makes the peanut mixture easier to shape.

PER BALL: 94 cal., 6 g total fat (2 g sat. fat), 1 mg chol., 76 mg sodium, 9 g carb., 1 g fiber, 2 g pro. Exchanges: 0.5 carb., 1 fat. Carb choices: 0.5.

¹/₃ **cup chunky peanut butter**

¹/₄ **cup 68 percent vegetable oil spread**

2 **tablespoons honey**

1 **cup rice and wheat cereal flakes, crushed slightly**

1 **cup bran flakes, crushed slightly**

¹/₃ **cup finely snipped dried apples**

2 **tablespoons finely chopped peanuts**

¹/₈ **teaspoon apple pie spice**

2 **ounces white baking chocolate (with cocoa butter), chopped**

¹/₄ **teaspoon shortening**

1. In a medium saucepan, combine peanut butter, vegetable oil spread, and honey. Cook over low heat just until melted and nearly smooth, whisking constantly. Stir in rice and wheat cereal flakes, bran flakes, apples, peanuts, and apple pie spice until mixed.

2. Divide cereal mixture into 18 portions. Using slightly wet hands, shape the cereal mixture into balls. Let stand on a waxed paper-lined baking sheet about 15 minutes or until firm.

3. In a small saucepan, combine white chocolate and shortening. Cook over low heat until melted, stirring constantly. Drizzle balls with melted white chocolate. Let stand about 15 minutes or until white chocolate is set (if necessary, chill balls until white chocolate is firm). Makes 18 balls.

slow-cooker meals

**Bloody Mary
Pot Roast**

Invite a handy slow cooker to your next party or family gathering. Use it to simmer one of our delicious entrees while you join the fun. When the stove top and oven are full, you'll have an extra cook station. And it's great for keeping hot foods hot on the buffet table.

Bloody Mary Pot Roast

Worchestershire sauce and spicy tomato juice create a robust sauce for this beef roast.

PER SERVING: 180 cal., 5 g total fat (2 g sat. fat), 81 mg chol., 255 mg sodium, 2 g carb., 0 g fiber, 29 g pro. Exchanges: 4 very lean meat, 1 fat. Carb choices: 0.

1   3- to 3 $\frac{1}{2}$-pound boneless beef chuck pot roast
$\frac{3}{4}$ cup hot-style tomato juice
1/4   cup water
1   teaspoon Worcestershire sauce
2   cloves garlic, minced
2   tablespoons cold water
4   teaspoons cornstarch
1   tablespoon prepared horseradish

1. Trim fat from meat and place meat in a 3$\frac{1}{2}$-quart slow cooker.

2. In a small bowl, combine tomato juice, the $\frac{1}{4}$ cup water, the Worcestershire sauce, and garlic; pour over meat in cooker.

3. Cover and cook on low-heat setting for 10 to 12 hours or on high-heat setting for 5 to 6 hours.

4. Reserve cooking liquid. Slice meat; transfer to a serving platter and cover to keep warm.

5. For gravy, pour 1$\frac{1}{2}$ cups of the cooking liquid into a small saucepan. Combine the 2 tablespoons cold water and the cornstarch; stir into the 1$\frac{1}{2}$ cups reserved cooking liquid. Cook and stir over medium heat until thickened and bubbly. Cook and stir for 2 minutes more. Stir in horseradish. Serve gravy with the meat. Makes 10 servings.

Dijon-Pepper Steak

Your guests will love this one-dish meal because it's tasty. You'll love it bcause it's easy.

PER SERVING: 275 cal., 9 g total fat (3 g sat. fat), 65 mg chol., 410 mg sodium, 10 g carb., 1 g fiber, 34 g pro. Exchanges: 4.5 lean meat, 1 vegetable. Carb choices: 0.5.

2 pounds boneless beef sirloin steak, cut 1 inch thick
1 to 1^1/$_2$ teaspoons cracked black pepper
1 tablespoon cooking oil
2 cups packaged whole trimmed baby carrots
1 medium onion, sliced
1 10^3/$_4$-ounce can reduced-fat and reduced-sodium condensed cream of celery soup
2 tablespoons Dijon-style mustard
3 cups hot cooked penne pasta (optional)
   Snipped fresh parsley (optional)

1. Trim fat from meat. Cut meat into six pieces. Sprinkle pepper evenly over meat; press in with your fingers. In a large skillet, brown meat, half at a time, in hot oil. Drain off fat. Set meat aside.

2. In a 3^1/$_2$- or 4-quart slow cooker, place carrots and onion. Add meat. In a medium bowl, stir together celery soup and Dijon-style mustard. Pour over mixture in slow cooker.

3. Cover and cook on low-heat setting for 7 to 8 hours or on high-heat setting for 3^1/$_2$ to 4 hours. If desired, before serving, use a fork to slightly break up steak pieces. If desired, serve over hot pasta and garnish with parsley. Makes 6 servings (about 3 ounces meat and scant ^{1}/$_2$ cup sauce-vegetable mixture per serving).

Spiced Pork Stew

Cinnamon, cumin, and ginger evoke a Moroccan flavor.

PER SERVING: 245 cal., 9 g total fat (3 g sat. fat), 51 mg chol., 530 mg sodium, 22 g carb., 3 g fiber, 17 g pro. Exchanges: 1 starch, 1.5 medium-fat meat, 1.5 vegetable. Carb choices: 1.5.

- 3 tablespoons all-purpose flour
- 1 teaspoon ground cumin
- 2 pounds boneless pork shoulder, cut into $^3/_4$-inch pieces
- 1 medium onion, chopped
- 2 tablespoons cooking oil
- 2 medium carrots, sliced
- 2 medium red potatoes, chopped
- 1 medium sweet potato, peeled and chopped
- 2 14.5-ounce cans diced tomatoes, undrained
- $^1/_3$ cup water
- 1 teaspoon salt
- 1 teaspoon ground ginger
- 1 teaspoon ground cinnamon
- $^1/_2$ teaspoon sugar
- $^1/_2$ teaspoon ground black pepper
- 2 cups loose-pack frozen cut green beans
- 2 tablespoons snipped fresh cilantro or parsley
- $^1/_2$ cup plain low-fat yogurt (optional)

1. In a large resealable plastic bag, combine flour and cumin. Add pork pieces to plastic bag; shake to coat. In a 4- to 5-quart Dutch oven, cook meat and onion, half at a time, in hot oil over medium heat until meat is brown. Drain off fat.

2. In a 4- to 5$^1/_2$-quart slow cooker, combine carrots, red potatoes, and sweet potato; top with pork mixture. Combine tomatoes, water, salt, ginger, cinnamon, sugar, and pepper; pour over pork.

3. Cover and cook on low-heat setting for 8 to 10 hours or on high-heat setting for 4 to 5 hours, adding green beans for the last 30 minutes.

4. To serve, top each serving with cilantro and, if desired, yogurt. Makes 8 (1$^1/_4$-cup) servings.

Quick Tip

Use your slow cooker to cook ahead for special meals. For the best flavor, freeze soups, stews, and meat dishes with gravy for up to 3 months. Meats with vegetables and pasta can be frozen for up to 1 month. To prevent freezer burn, store the food in freezer containers with tightly fitting lids.

Spiced Pork Stew

Cider Pork Stew

Cider Pork Stew

Apple cider lends a subtle sweetness to this hearty stew.

PER SERVING: 272 cal., 7 g total fat (2 g sat. fat), 73 mg chol., 405 mg sodium, 27 g carb., 3 g fiber, 24 g pro. Exchanges: 1 starch, 0.5 fruit, 3 very lean meat, 0.5 vegetable, 1 fat. Carb choices: 2

- 2 pounds pork shoulder roast
- 3 medium potatoes, cubed (about 2¹/₂ cups)
- 3 medium carrots, cut into ¹/₂-inch pieces (about 1¹/₂ cups)
- 2 medium onions, sliced
- 1 medium apple, cored and coarsely chopped (1 cup)
- ¹/₂ cup coarsely chopped celery
- 2 cups apple cider or apple juice
- 3 tablespoons quick-cooking tapioca
- 1 teaspoon salt
- 1 teaspoon caraway seeds
- ¹/₄ teaspoon ground black pepper
  Celery leaves (optional)

1. Trim fat from meat; cut meat into 1-inch cubes. In a 3¹/₂- to 5¹/₂-quart slow cooker, combine meat, potatoes, carrots, onions, apple, and celery. In a glass measuring cup, stir together apple juice, tapioca, salt, caraway, and pepper; pour over meat and vegetables.

2. Cover and cook on low-heat setting for 10 to 12 hours or high-heat setting for 5 to 6 hours.

3. To serve, spoon into 8 soup bowls. If desired, garnish with celery leaves. Makes 8 (1-cup) servings.

Shredded Pork Sandwiches

This recipe feeds a crowd. Cut carbs by skipping the bun.

PER SANDWICH: 270 cal., 10 g total fat (3 g sat. fat), 55 mg chol., 500 mg sodium, 24 g carb., 2 g fiber, 22 g pro. Exchanges: 1.5 starch, 2.5 lean meat, 0.5 vegetable. Carb choices: 1.5.

- 1¹/₂ teaspoons garlic powder
- 1¹/₂ teaspoons onion powder
- 1¹/₂ teaspoons ground black pepper
- 1 teaspoon celery salt
- 1 3-pound boneless pork shoulder roast
- 2 large onions, cut into thin wedges
- ¹/₂ cup water
- 2 cups packaged shredded broccoli (broccoli slaw mix)
- 1 cup light mayonnaise dressing or salad dressing
- 16 whole grain hamburger buns

Shredded Pork Sandwiches

1. In a small bowl, stir together garlic powder, onion powder, pepper, and celery salt. Trim fat from meat. Sprinkle garlic powder mixture evenly onto meat; rub into meat with your fingers. If necessary, cut meat to fit into a 3¹/₂- or 4-quart slow cooker.

2. Place onions in slow cooker. Add meat and water. Cover and cook on low-heat setting for 8 to 10 hours or on high-heat setting for 4 to 5 hours.

3. Using a slotted spoon, transfer meat to a cutting board; discard cooking liquid. Using two forks, shred meat. Return meat to slow cooker to keep warm.

4. To serve, in a small bowl, combine broccoli and ¹/₄ cup of the mayonnaise dressing. Spread cut sides of buns with remaining dressing. Spoon meat onto bun bottoms. Top with broccoli mixture and bun tops. Makes 16 sandwiches.

Pork Primavera Sandwiches

A purchased barbecue sauce not only makes these sandwiches a cinch to put together but also gives you the flexibility to choose the flavor profile.

PER SANDWICH: 258 cal., 5 g total fat (1 g sat. fat), 57 mg chol., 418 mg sodium, 28 g carb., 3 g fiber, 24 g pro. Exchanges: 2 starch, 2.5 medium-fat meat. Carb choices: 2.

- 2 medium carrots, shredded (about 1 cup)
- 1 large red sweet pepper, seeded and coarsely chopped
- 1 medium onion, cut into thin wedges
- 2 tablespoons quick-cooking tapioca, crushed
- 2 to 2¹/₂ pounds boneless pork sirloin roast or boneless pork loin roast, trimmed of fat
- ³/₄ cup bottled reduced-sodium, fat-free barbecue sauce
- 10 whole wheat hamburger buns, split and toasted

1. In a 3¹/₂- or 4-quart slow cooker, combine carrots, sweet pepper, and onion. Sprinkle with tapioca. Place meat on top of vegetables. Pour barbecue sauce over meat.

2. Cover and cook on low-heat setting for 6 to 7 hours or on high-heat setting for 3 to 3¹/₂ hours.

3. Remove meat from slow cooker, reserving juices. Thinly slice meat. Return meat to slow cooker; stir to coat with sauce. Serve meat on buns. Makes 10 sandwiches.

Spicy Pork Sandwiches

No need to wait until summer to serve a barbecued sandwich. Let your slow cooker do the honors. Serve with coleslaw for a real Southern accent.

PER SANDWICH: 292 cal., 7 g total fat (2 g sat. fat), 79 mg chol., 402 mg sodium, 23 g carb., 1 g fiber, 31 g pro. Exchanges: 1.5 starch, 3.5 lean meat. Carb choices: 1.5.

- 1 2¹/₂- to 3-pound pork sirloin roast
- ¹/₂ teaspoon garlic powder
- ¹/₂ teaspoon ground ginger
- ¹/₂ teaspoon dried thyme, crushed
- 1 cup chicken broth
- ¹/₂ cup vinegar
- ¹/₂ teaspoon cayenne pepper
- 8 to 10 hamburger buns, split and toasted

1. Remove string from roast, if present. Trim fat from roast. If necessary, cut roast to fit into a 3¹/₂- to 4-quart slow cooker. In a small bowl, combine garlic powder, ginger, and thyme. Sprinkle garlic powder mixture over roast. Using your fingers, rub mixture into meat. Place roast in cooker. Pour broth over roast.

2. Cover and cook on low-heat setting for 8 to 10 hours or on high-heat setting for 4 to 5 hours.

3. Remove meat from cooker, reserving cooking liquid. Using two forks, shred meat and place in a large bowl. Add 1 cup of the cooking liquid, the vinegar, and cayenne pepper to meat in bowl; toss to combine. Serve on buns. Makes 8 to 10 sandwiches.

Barbecued Turkey Thighs

Who needs a grill for barbecue? These saucy turkey thighs hold their form nicely during slow cooking and can hold their own among other grilled turkey dishes.

PER SERVING: 225 cal., 6 g total fat (2 g sat. fat), 100 mg chol., 444 mg sodium, 12 g carb., 1 g fiber, 30 g pro. Exchanges: 1 carb., 4 very lean meat, 1 fat. Carb choices: 1.

 $^1/_2$ cup ketchup
 2 tablespoons sugar substitute*
 1 tablespoon quick-cooking tapioca
 1 tablespoon vinegar
 1 teaspoon Worcestershire sauce
 $^1/_4$ teaspoon ground cinnamon
 $^1/_4$ teaspoon crushed red pepper
 2 to 2$^1/_2$ pounds turkey thighs (about 2 thighs) or meaty chicken pieces (breasts, thighs, and drumsticks), skinned
   Hot cooked brown rice or whole wheat pasta (optional)

1. In a 3$^1/_2$- or 4-quart slow cooker, combine ketchup, sugar substitute, tapioca, vinegar, Worcestershire sauce, cinnamon, and red pepper. Place turkey thighs, meaty sides down, on ketchup mixture.

2. Cover and cook on low-heat setting for 10 to 12 hours or high-heat setting for 5 to 6 hours. Transfer turkey to a serving dish. Pour cooking juices into a small bowl; skim off fat. Serve turkey with cooking juices and, if desired, hot cooked rice. Makes 4 to 6 servings.

***Sugar Substitutes:** Choose from Splenda granular, Equal Spoonful or packets, or Sweet'N Low bulk or packets.

Sesame-Ginger Turkey Wraps

Need a party theme? Go Asian with these wraps. Don't forget fortune cookies!

PER WRAP: 207 cal., 5 g total fat (1 g sat. fat), 67 mg chol., 422 mg sodium, 20 g carb., 2 g fiber, 20 g pro. Exchanges: 1 vegetable, 1 starch, 2 lean meat. Carb choices: 1.5.

   Nonstick cooking spray
 3 **turkey thighs, skinned (3$^1/_2$ to 4 pounds total)**
 1 **cup bottled sesame-ginger stir-fry sauce**
 $^1/_4$ **cup water**
 1 **16-ounce package shredded broccoli (broccoli slaw mix)**
 12 **8-inch flour tortillas, warmed***
 $^3/_4$ **cup sliced green onions**

1. Lightly coat a 3$^1/_2$- or 4-quart slow cooker with cooking spray. Place turkey thighs in slow cooker. In a small bowl, stir together stir-fry sauce and the water. Pour over turkey.

2. Cover and cook on low-heat setting for 6 to 7 hours or on high-heat setting for 3 to 3$^1/_2$ hours.

3. Remove turkey from slow cooker; cool slightly. Remove turkey from bones; discard bones. Using two forks, pull turkey apart into shreds.

4. Meanwhile, place broccoli in the sauce mixture in the slow cooker; stir to coat. Cover and let stand for 5 minutes. Using a slotted spoon, remove broccoli from slow cooker.

5. To assemble, place some of the turkey on each tortilla. Top with broccoli mixture and green onions. Spoon sauce from slow cooker on top of green onions. Roll up. Serve immediately. Makes 12 wraps.

***Test Kitchen Tip:** To warm tortillas, wrap them in white microwave-safe paper towels; microwave on 100 percent power (high) for 15 to 30 seconds or until tortillas are softened. (Or preheat oven to 350°F. Wrap tortillas in foil. Heat for 10 to 15 minutes or until warmed.)

Spinach, Chicken, and Wild Rice Soup

Chicken and Shrimp Jambalaya

Removing the skin from a chicken breast half saves about 6 grams of fat and 50 calories per serving.

PER SERVING: 211 cal., 2 g total fat (0 g sat. fat), 88 mg chol., 415 mg sodium, 26 g carb., 4 g fiber, 23 g pro. Exchanges: 1 starch, 1.5 vegetable, 2.5 very lean meat. Carb choices: 2.

- 2 cups thinly sliced celery
- 2 cups chopped onions
- 1 14.5-ounce can no-salt-added diced tomatoes
- 1 14-ounce can reduced-sodium chicken broth
- $1/2$ of a 6-ounce can ($1/3$ cup) no-salt-added tomato paste
- 2 cloves garlic, minced
- 1 recipe Homemade Salt-Free Cajun Seasoning (see recipe, below) or salt-free Cajun seasoning
- $1/2$ teaspoon salt
- 1 pound skinless, boneless chicken breast halves or thighs, cut into $3/4$-inch pieces
- $1^1/2$ cups instant brown rice
- $3/4$ cup chopped green, red, and/or yellow sweet pepper
- 8 ounces cooked peeled and deveined shrimp, tails intact
- 2 tablespoons snipped fresh parsley
  Celery leaves (optional)

1. In a $3^1/2$- or 4-quart slow cooker, stir together celery, onions, undrained tomatoes, broth, tomato paste, garlic, Cajun seasoning, and salt. Stir in chicken.

2. Cover and cook on low-heat setting for $4^1/2$ to $5^1/2$ hours or on high-heat setting for $2^1/4$ to $2^3/4$ hours.

3. If using low-heat setting, turn to high-heat setting. Stir in uncooked rice and sweet pepper. Cover; cook about 30 minutes more or until most of the liquid is absorbed and rice is tender.

4. Stir in shrimp and parsley. If desired, garnish with celery leaves. Makes 8 ($1^1/2$-cup) servings.

Homemade Salt-Free Cajun Seasoning: Stir together $1/4$ teaspoon each ground white pepper, garlic powder, onion powder, paprika, and ground black pepper and $1/8$ to $1/4$ teaspoon cayenne pepper.

Spinach, Chicken, and Wild Rice Soup

Here's a perfect—and delicious—way to use leftovers from that long holiday meal.

PER SERVING: 216 cal., 4 g total fat (1 g sat. fat), 64 mg chol., 397 mg sodium, 19 g carb., 2 g fiber, 26 g pro. Exchanges: 1 starch, 3 very lean meat, 0.5 vegetable, 0.5 fat. Carb choices: 1.

- 3 cups water
- 1 14-ounce can reduced-sodium chicken broth
- 1 10.75-ounce can reduced-fat and reduced-sodium condensed cream of chicken soup
- $2/3$ cup wild rice, rinsed and drained
- $1/2$ teaspoon dried thyme, crushed
- $1/4$ teaspoon ground black pepper
- 3 cups chopped cooked chicken or turkey (about 1 pound)
- 2 cups chopped fresh spinach

1. In a $3^1/2$- or 4-quart slow cooker, combine the water, broth, condensed cream of chicken soup, uncooked wild rice, thyme, and pepper.

2. Cover and cook on low-heat setting for 7 to 8 hours or on high-heat setting for $3^1/2$ to 4 hours.

3. To serve, stir in chicken and spinach. Makes 6 ($1^1/2$-cup) servings.

Chicken, Barley, and Leek Stew

Freeze this stew up to 3 months in advance for a quick
meal when you're busy with holiday activities.

PER SERVING: 248 cal., 6 g total fat (1 g sat. fat), 63 mg chol., 558 mg
sodium, 27 g carb., 6 g fiber, 22 g pro. Exchanges: 0.5 vegetable,
1.5 starch, 2.5 lean meat. Carb choices: 2.

1 **pound skinless, boneless chicken thighs, cut into
1-inch pieces**
1 **tablespoon olive oil**
3 **14-ounce cans reduced-sodium chicken broth**
3/4 **cups water**

1 **cup regular barley (not quick-cooking)**
3 **medium leeks, halved lengthwise and sliced**
2 **medium carrots, thinly sliced**
1 1/2 **teaspoons dried thyme or Italian seasoning, crushed**
1/4 **teaspoon cracked black pepper**

1. In a large skillet, cook chicken in hot oil until brown.
In a 4- to 5-quart slow cooker, combine chicken, broth,
water, barley, leeks, carrots, thyme, and pepper.

2. Cover and cook stew on low-heat setting for 4 to
5 hours or on high-heat setting for 2 to 2 1/2 hours or until
barley is tender. Makes 6 (1 1/2-cup) servings.

**Chicken, Barley,
and Leek Stew**

Teriyaki and Orange Chicken

This sauce is sweet and full of flavor. Use orange sections or slices for a colorful garnish.

PER SERVING: 320 cal., 2 g total fat (0 g sat. fat), 66 mg chol., 432 mg sodium, 41 g carb., 5 g fiber, 32 g pro. Exchanges: 1 vegetable, 1.5 starch, 1 other carb., 3 lean meat. Carb choices: 3.

- **1 16-ounce package frozen loose-pack broccoli, carrots, and water chestnuts**
- **2 tablespoons quick-cooking tapioca**
- **1 pound skinless, boneless chicken breast halves or thighs, cut into 1-inch pieces**
- **³/4 cup reduced-sodium chicken broth**
- **3 tablespoons low-sugar orange marmalade**
- **2 tablespoons bottled light teriyaki sauce**
- **1 teaspoon dry mustard**
- **¹/2 teaspoon ground ginger**
- **2 cups hot cooked brown rice**

1. In a 3¹/2- or 4-quart slow cooker, combine frozen vegetables and tapioca. Add chicken.

2. In a small bowl, combine chicken broth, orange marmalade, teriyaki sauce, dry mustard, and ginger. Pour over mixture in cooker.

3. Cover and cook on low-heat setting for 4 to 5 hours or on high-heat setting for 2 to 2¹/2 hours. Serve with hot cooked rice. Makes 4 servings.

Rosemary Chicken and Artichokes

Artichokes give some class to everyday chicken. Slow cooking gives you time with guests.

PER SERVING: 168 cal., 4 g total fat (1 g sat. fat), 89 mg chol., 328 mg sodium, 8 g carb., 3 g fiber, 23 g pro. Exchanges: 3 very lean meat, 1.5 vegetable, 0.5 fat. Carb choices: 0.5.

1 **medium onion, chopped**
6 **cloves garlic, minced**
$1/3$ **cup reduced-sodium chicken broth**
1 **tablespoon quick-cooking tapioca**
2 to 3 **teaspoons finely shredded lemon peel**
2 **teaspoons snipped fresh rosemary or 1 teaspoon dried rosemary, crushed**
$3/4$ **teaspoon ground black pepper**
$2^1/2$ to 3 **pounds chicken thighs, skinned**
$1/2$ **teaspoon salt**
1 **8- or 9-ounce package frozen artichoke hearts, thawed**
1 **medium red sweet pepper, cut into strips**
Hot cooked brown rice (optional)
Snipped fresh parsley (optional)
Fresh rosemary sprigs (optional)

1. In a $3^1/2$- to 4-quart slow cooker, combine onion, garlic, broth, tapioca, 1 teaspoon of the lemon peel, the snipped rosemary, and $1/2$ teaspoon of the black pepper. Add chicken. Sprinkle with salt and remaining $1/4$ teaspoon black pepper.

2. Cover and cook on low-heat setting for 5 to 6 hours or on high-heat setting for $2^1/2$ to 3 hours.

3. If using low-heat setting, turn cooker to high heat. Add thawed artichokes and pepper strips. Cover; cook for 30 minutes more.

4. To serve, top with remaining 1 to 2 teaspoons lemon peel. If desired, serve with cooked brown rice, sprinkle with parsley, and garnish with rosemary sprigs. Makes 6 servings.

Italian Chicken and Pasta

Use spinach or red pepper fettuccine—or both—for a yuletide dish.

PER SERVING: 383 cal., 6 g total fat (2 g sat. fat), 73 mg chol., 392 mg sodium, 52 g carb., 7 g fiber, 28 g pro. Exchanges: 3.5 vegetable, 2 starch, 3 lean meat. Carb choices: 3.5.

12 **ounces skinless, boneless chicken thighs**
1 **9-ounce package frozen Italian-style green beans**
1 **cup fresh mushrooms, quartered**
1 **small onion, sliced $1/4$ inch thick**
1 **14.5-ounce can Italian-style stewed tomatoes, undrained**
1 **6-ounce can no-salt-added tomato paste**
$1^1/2$ **teaspoon dried Italian seasoning, crushed**
2 **cloves garlic, minced**
6 **ounces wide egg noodles, cooked and drained**
3 **tablespoons finely shredded Parmesan cheese (optional)**

1. Cut chicken into 1-inch pieces; set aside. In a $3^1/2$- or 4-quart slow cooker, place green beans, mushrooms, and onion. Place chicken on vegetables.

2. In a bowl, combine undrained tomatoes, tomato paste, Italian seasoning, and garlic. Pour over chicken.

3. Cover and cook on low-heat setting for 5 to 6 hours or on high-heat setting for $2^1/2$ to 3 hours. Serve over hot cooked pasta. If desired, sprinkle with Parmesan cheese. Makes 4 ($1^1/2$-cup) servings.

Chicken in Wine Sauce

1. In a 5- or 6-quart slow cooker, place potatoes, carrots, celery, and onion. Place chicken pieces on top of vegetables. Sprinkle with parsley, salt, rosemary, thyme, pepper, and garlic; add broth and wine.

2. Cover and cook on low-heat setting for 8 to 9 hours or on high-heat setting for 4 to $4^1/_2$ hours. Using a slotted spoon, transfer chicken and vegetables to a serving platter; cover with foil to keep warm.

3. For gravy, skim fat from cooking juices; strain juices. In a large saucepan, melt butter. Stir in flour and cook for 1 minute. Add cooking juices. Cook and stir until thickened and bubbly. Cook and stir 2 minutes more. If desired, sprinkle chicken and vegetables with snipped thyme. Pass gravy with the chicken and vegetables. Makes 6 servings.

Zesty Ginger-Tomato Chicken

Chicken drumsticks or thighs stay moist and tender during the slow cooker's long cooking time.

PER SERVING: 302 cal., 6 g total fat (1 g sat. fat), 81 mg chol., 549 mg sodium, 35 g carb., 4 g fiber, 28 g pro. Exchanges: 1 vegetable, 2 starch, 3 very lean meat, 0.5 fat. Carb choices: 2.5.

- $2^1/_2$ to 3 pounds skinless chicken drumsticks and/or thighs
- 2 14.5-ounce cans diced tomatoes
- 2 tablespoons quick-cooking tapioca
- 1 tablespoon grated fresh ginger
- 1 tablespoon snipped fresh cilantro or parsley
- 4 cloves garlic, minced
- $^1/_2$ teaspoon crushed red pepper
- $^1/_2$ teaspoon salt
- 3 cups hot cooked quinoa or brown rice

1. Place chicken in a $3^1/_2$- or 4-quart slow cooker. Drain 1 can tomatoes. In a medium bowl, combine drained and undrained tomatoes, the tapioca, ginger, cilantro, garlic, red pepper, and salt. Pour over chicken.

2. Cover and cook on low-heat setting for 6 to 7 hours or on high-heat setting for 3 to $3^1/_2$ hours.

3. Remove chicken from cooker; skim fat from liquid. Serve with hot cooked quinoa. Makes 6 servings.

Chicken in Wine Sauce

Chicken in Wine Sauce

Chicken and hearty vegetables simmer in a delicate wine-flavored sauce. Choose dark meat chicken—legs, thighs, or drumsticks—for this classy dish.

PER SERVING: 328 cal., 11 g total fat (5 g sat. fat), 124 mg chol., 544 mg sodium, 24 g carb., 3 g fiber, 29 g pro. Exchanges: 0.5 vegetable, 1.5 starch, 3.5 lean meat. Carb choices: 1.5.

- 4 medium red-skin potatoes, quartered
- 4 medium carrots, cut into $^1/_2$-inch pieces
- 2 stalks celery, cut into 1-inch pieces
- 1 small onion, sliced
- 3 pounds chicken thighs or drumsticks, skinned
- 1 tablespoon snipped fresh parsley
- $^1/_2$ teaspoon salt
- $^1/_2$ teaspoon dried rosemary, crushed
- $^1/_2$ teaspoon dried thyme, crushed
- $^1/_4$ teaspoon ground black pepper
- 1 clove garlic, minced
- 1 cup chicken broth
- $^1/_2$ cup dry white wine
- 3 tablespoons butter or margarine
- 3 tablespoons all-purpose flour
  Snipped fresh thyme (optional)

(trim and skim)

Slow cooking requires little fat, thanks to low, moist heat. For even lower-fat meals, choose lean cuts of meat and trim away as much visible fat as possible. For poultry, remove the skin before cooking. Brown the meat in a nonstick skillet coated with cooking spray. Before serving the meal, use a slotted spoon to transfer the meat and vegetables to a serving platter. Pour the cooking liquid into a glass measuring cup and let it stand for a couple of minutes. Once the fat rises to the top, skim off any visible fat with a metal spoon.

Zesty Ginger-Tomato Chicken

(storage safety)

For safety reasons, food should not be left in slow cookers to cool after cooking. Also, don't use slow cookers as storage containers or place them in the refrigerator. To properly store cooked food, remove food from the cooker. (If the food is very hot, transfer it to a large, shallow container to cool.) After it has sufficiently cooled (leave for no longer than 2 hours at room temperature), transfer the food to refrigerator or freezer storage containers. Cover tightly; label and date the containers.

Chicken Gumbo

Chicken Gumbo

Roux ("rue") is generally a mixture of flour and fat that is cooked until very brown and used as a thickener. Here, the flour is browned alone and broth replaces the fat.

PER SERVING: 230 cal., 5 g total fat (1 g sat. fat), 48 mg chol., 425 mg sodium, 27 g carb., 3 g fiber, 19 g pro. Exchanges: 0.5 vegetable, 1.5 starch, 2 lean meat. Carb choices: 2.

$^1/_3$ cup all-purpose flour
  1 14-ounce can reduced-sodium chicken broth
  2 cups chopped cooked chicken breast or turkey breast (10 ounces)
  8 ounces smoked turkey sausage links, quartered lengthwise and sliced
  2 cups sliced fresh okra or one 10-ounce package frozen cut okra, partially thawed
  1 cup water
  1 cup coarsely chopped onion
  1 cup coarsely chopped red or green sweet pepper
$^1/_2$ cup sliced celery
  4 cloves garlic, minced
  1 teaspoon dried thyme, crushed
$^1/_2$ teaspoon ground black pepper
$^1/_4$ teaspoon cayenne pepper
  3 cups hot cooked brown rice

1. For roux, in a heavy medium saucepan, cook flour over medium heat about 6 minutes or until brown, stirring occasionally. Remove from heat; cool slightly. Gradually stir broth into flour. Cook and stir until thickened and bubbly.

2. Pour the roux into a 3 $^1/_2$- or 4-quart slow cooker. Add the chicken, sausage links, okra, the water, onion, sweet pepper, celery, garlic, thyme, black pepper, and cayenne pepper.

3. Cover and cook on low-heat setting for 6 to 7 hours or high-heat setting for 3 to 3 $^1/_2$ hours. Skim off fat. Serve gumbo over cooked brown rice. Makes 8 servings ($^3/_4$ cup soup plus $^1/_3$ cup rice).

Brown Rice Risotto with Lamb

Celebrate spring with a one-pot meal of curried lamb and healthful brown rice.

PER SERVING: 257 cal., 6 g total fat (2 g sat. fat), 72 mg chol., 375 mg sodium, 23 g carb., 2 g fiber, 25 g pro. Exchanges: 1 vegetable, 1 starch, 3 very lean meat, 1 fat. Carb choices: 1.5.

1 **2- to 2^1/$_2$-pound (boneless) lamb shoulder roast**
   Nonstick cooking spray
2^1/$_2$ **cups hot-style vegetable juice**
1 **cup brown rice**
1 **teaspoon curry powder**
^{1}/$_4$ **teaspoon salt**
2 **medium carrots, chopped**
^{3}/$_4$ **cup chopped green sweet pepper**

1. Trim fat from meat. If necessary, cut meat to fit into a 3^1/$_2$- or 4-quart slow cooker. Coat an unheated large nonstick skillet with cooking spray. Preheat skillet over medium heat. Cook meat in hot skillet until brown, turning to brown evenly. Drain off fat.

2. In the slow cooker, combine vegetable juice, uncooked brown rice, curry powder, and salt. Top with carrots. Place meat on top of carrots.

3. Cover and cook on low-heat setting for 8 to 9 hours or on high-heat setting for 4 to 4^1/$_2$ hours.

4. Add sweet pepper. Cover; let stand for 5 to 10 minutes or until pepper is tender. Makes 8 servings.

Spicy Steak and Beans

Spicy Steak and Beans

Queso fresco (KAY-so FRESK-o) means "fresh cheese" in Spanish. Look for it in Mexican or larger supermarkets.

PER SERVING: 262 cal., 8 g total fat (3 g sat. fat), 45 mg chol., 452 mg sodium, 17 g carb., 4 g fiber, 29 g pro. Exchanges: 1 vegetable, 1 starch, 3.5 very lean meat, 1 fat. Carb choices: 1.

- 1^1/$_2$ pounds beef flank steak
- 1 10-ounce can chopped tomatoes with green chile peppers, undrained
- ^{1}/$_2$ cup chopped onion
- 2 cloves garlic, minced
- 1 tablespoon snipped fresh oregano or 1 teaspoon dried oregano, crushed
- 1 teaspoon chili powder
- 1 teaspoon ground cumin
- ^{1}/$_4$ teaspoon salt
- ^{1}/$_4$ teaspoon ground black pepper
- 2 small green, red, and/or yellow sweet peppers, cut into strips
- 1 15-ounce can pinto beans, rinsed and drained
  Hot cooked brown rice (optional)
  Crumbled queso fresco or feta cheese (optional)

1. Trim fat from meat. Place meat in a 3^1/$_2$- or 4-quart slow cooker. In a bowl, stir together undrained tomatoes, onion, garlic, dried oregano (if using), chili powder, cumin, salt, and black pepper. Pour over meat.

2. Cover and cook on low-heat setting for 7 to 9 hours or on high-heat setting for 3^1/$_2$ to 4^1/$_2$ hours.

3. If using low-heat setting, turn to high-heat setting. Stir in sweet pepper strips and pinto beans. Cover and cook for 30 minutes. Remove meat; cool slightly. Shred or thinly slice meat across the grain. Stir fresh oregano (if using) into bean mixture.

4. If using, spoon rice into soup bowls. Arrange meat on top of rice. Spoon bean mixture over meat. If desired, sprinkle with queso fresco. Makes 6 (1-cup) servings.

Quick Tip

Home-cooked dried beans offer all the nutrients of canned beans without all the sodium. When you have time, cook dried beans and freeze them in 2-cup portions. When a recipe calls for a 15-ounce can of beans, thaw a container of cooked beans to use instead.

Supersimple Beef Stew

Enjoy this delicious stew after cold outdoor activites. Entertaining has never been so easy.

PER SERVING: 365 cal., 13 g total fat (0 g sat. fat), 54 mg chol., 830 mg sodium, 32 g carb., 6 g fiber, 31 g pro. Exchanges: 1.5 vegetable, 1.5 starch, 3 .5 lean meat, 0.5 fat. Carb choices: 2.

- 12 ounces small red potatoes, quartered (about 2 cups)
- 4 medium carrots, cut into ^{1}/$_2$-inch pieces
- 1 small red onion, cut into wedges
- 1 pound beef stew meat
- 1 10.75-ounce can condensed cream of mushroom or cream of celery soup
- 1 cup beef broth
- ^{1}/$_2$ teaspoon dried marjoram or dried thyme, crushed
- 1 9-ounce package frozen cut green beans, thawed

1. In a 3^1/$_2$- or 4-quart slow cooker, place potatoes, carrots, onion, stew meat, soup, beef broth, and marjoram. Stir to combine.

2. Cover and cook on low-heat setting for 8 to 9 hours or on high-heat setting for 4 to 4^1/$_2$ hours.

3. If using low-heat setting, turn to high-heat setting. Stir in thawed green beans. Cover and cook for 10 to 15 minutes more or just until green beans are tender. Makes 4 (1^3/$_4$-cup) servings.

Supersimple Beef Stew

(10 slow cooker tips)

Using your slow cooker saves time, but you can do more to make it more efficient and safe.

1. **Check** that your cooker is the right size for the recipe you're making.
2. **Make sure** your cooker is at least half full but no more than two-thirds full so foods cook safely in the given time range.
3. **Look** for do-ahead steps. Can you cook the meat or cut up the vegetables the night before?
4. **Cut vegetables** into suggested sizes. Slower-cooking vegetables may need to be cut into smaller pieces than quicker-cooking vegetables.
5. **Don't add or delete** ingredients that will affect the volume or cooking time.
6. **Don't peek!** Although it's tempting to lift the lid, resist. You'll lose heat and prolong cooking time.
7. **Keep it simple.** Toss a salad with a low-calorie dressing to serve alongside.
8. **To thicken a sauce in your cooker,** remove the meat and vegetables with a slotted spoon from the liner and keep them warm in the oven.
9. **Transfer leftovers** to airtight containers to cool or freeze. Don't reheat them in your cooker.
10. **Add a little water** and dish detergent to the liner when empty. Wash and dry the liner completely.

(ground meat savvy)

Although you might think ground turkey and ground chicken are leaner alternatives to ground beef, beware. Some products contain dark meat and/or skin, which are not as lean as breast meat. When using ground chicken or turkey, look for the leanest meat you can find. If you can't find packages that are specifically labeled as breast meat only, ask the butcher to skin, bone, and grind chicken or turkey breasts for you or grind the meat yourself using a coarse blade in a food grinder.

Italian Wedding Soup

Italian Wedding Soup

To make even-size meatballs, pat the meat mixture into a 1-inch-thick square and cut into 12 even portions. Shape and continue as directed.

PER SERVING: 283 cal., 10 g total fat (3 g sat. fat.), 83 mg chol., 515 mg sodium, 26 g carb., 3 g fiber, 21 g pro. Exchanges: 1.5 starch, 2 lean meat, 1 vegetable, 1 fat. Carb choices: 2.

- **1** large onion
- **3** oil-packed dried tomatoes, finely snipped
- **2** teaspoons dried Italian seasoning, crushed
- **1** pound lean ground beef
- **1** egg, slightly beaten
- **1/4** cup fine dry bread crumbs
- **2** teaspoons olive oil
- **1** large fennel bulb
- **2** 14-ounce cans reduced-sodium chicken broth
- **3 1/2** cups water
- **6** cloves garlic, thinly sliced
- **1/2** teaspoon ground black pepper
- **3/4** cup dried orzo pasta
- **5** cups shredded fresh spinach

1. Finely chop one-third of the onion; thinly slice remaining onion. In a large bowl, combine chopped onion, dried tomatoes, and 1 teaspoon of the Italian seasoning. Add ground beef, egg, and bread crumbs; mix well. Shape into 12 meatballs.

2. In a large skillet, cook meatballs in hot oil over medium heat until brown, turning occasionally. Carefully drain off fat. Transfer meatballs to a 4 1/2- to 5-quart slow cooker.

3. Meanwhile, cut off and discard upper stalks of fennel. If desired, reserve some fennel leaves for a garnish. Remove any wilted outer layers; cut off a thin slice from fennel base. Cut fennel into thin wedges. Add fennel wedges, broth, water, garlic, remaining 1 teaspoon Italian seasoning, and the pepper to cooker.

4. Cover and cook on low-heat setting for 8 to 10 hours or on high-heat setting for 4 to 5 hours.

5. If using low-heat setting, turn cooker to high-heat setting. Gently stir orzo into soup. Cover; cook for 15 minutes. Stir in spinach. If desired, garnish soup with reserved fennel leaves. Makes 6 (1 2/3-cup) servings.

Fireside Beef Stew

Fireside Beef Stew

This stew cooks all day while you and your family play!

PER SERVING: 206 cal., 4 g total fat (1 g sat. fat), 67 mg chol., 440 mg sodium, 15 g carb., 3 g fiber, 27 g pro. Exchanges: 0.5 starch, 2.5 lean meat, 1.5 vegetable. Carb choices: 1.

- **1 1/2** pounds boneless beef chuck (pot) roast
- **1** pound butternut squash
- **2** small onions, cut into wedges
- **1** 14-ounce can lower-sodium beef broth
- **1** 8-ounce can tomato sauce
- **2** tablespoons Worcestershire sauce
- **2** cloves garlic, minced
- **1** teaspoon dry mustard
- **1/4** teaspoon ground black pepper
- **1/8** teaspoon ground allspice
- **2** tablespoons cold water
- **4** teaspoons cornstarch
- **1** 9-ounce package frozen Italian green beans

1. Trim fat from meat; cut into 1-inch pieces. Peel, seed, and cut squash into 1-inch pieces. In a 3 1/2- to 4 1/2-quart slow cooker, layer meat, squash, and onions. Add broth, tomato sauce, Worcestershire sauce, garlic, mustard, pepper, and allspice.

2. Cover and cook on low-heat setting for 8 to 10 hours or on high-heat setting for 4 to 5 hours.

3. For sauce, in a small bowl, stir together cold water and cornstarch; stir into cooker. Add green beans.

4. Cover and cook on high heat for 15 minutes or until thickened. Makes 6 (1 1/3-cup) servings.

Beef Soup with Root Vegetables

Beef Soup with Root Vegetables

This hearty soup brings warmth to a cold, blustery day.

PER SERVING: 167 cal., 2 g total fat (1 g sat. fat), 37 mg chol., 453 mg sodium, 14 g carb., 2 g fiber, 23 g pro. Exchanges: 1 starch, 2.5 very lean meat, 0.5 vegetable. Carb choices: 1.

$1^1/_2$ pounds boneless beef round steak
  Nonstick cooking spray
  2 stalks celery, sliced
  1 large onion, coarsely chopped
  1 medium carrot, sliced
  2 cloves garlic, minced
  2 medium potatoes, peeled and cut into $^3/_4$-inch cubes
  2 medium turnips, peeled and cut into $^3/_4$-inch cubes
  1 large sweet potato, peeled and cut into $^3/_4$-inch cubes
  3 14-ounce cans reduced-sodium beef broth
  1 cup water
  2 tablespoons snipped fresh thyme or 2 teaspoons dried thyme, crushed
  2 teaspoons Worcestershire sauce
$^1/_4$ teaspoon salt
$^1/_4$ teaspoon ground black pepper
  1 bay leaf

1. Trim fat from steak. Cut steak into $^3/_4$-inch cubes. Coat an unheated 4-quart Dutch oven with cooking spray. Preheat over medium-high heat. Cook meat, half at a time, in hot pan until brown.

2. In a $4^1/_2$- to 6-quart slow cooker, combine celery, onion, carrot, garlic, potatoes, turnips, and sweet potato. Add browned meat. In a medium bowl, combine broth, water, thyme, Worcestershire sauce, salt, pepper, and bay leaf; pour over beef.

3. Cover and cook on low-heat setting for 10 to 12 hours or on high-heat setting for 5 to 6 hours. Before serving, discard bay leaf. Makes 8 ($1^1/_4$-cup) servings.

Beef and Red Bean Chili

If you usually make chili with ground beef, try chunks of chuck. The beans add heart-healthy fiber.

PER SERVING: 298 cal., 7 g total fat (2 g sat. fat), 67 mg chol., 455 mg sodium, 26 g carb., 5 g fiber, 30 g pro. Exchanges: 1 starch, 2 vegetable, 3 lean meat, 1 fat. Carb choices: 2.

- 1 cup dry red beans or dry kidney beans
- 1 tablespoon olive oil
- 2 pounds boneless beef chuck pot roast, cut into 1-inch pieces
- 1 cup coarsely chopped onion (1 large)
- 1 15-ounce can no-salt-added tomato sauce
- 1 14.5-ounce can diced tomatoes with mild chiles, undrained
- 1 14-ounce can lower-sodium beef broth
- 1 or 2 chipotle peppers in adobo sauce, finely chopped; plus 2 teaspoons adobo sauce*
- 2 teaspoons dried oregano, crushed
- 1 teaspoon ground cumin
- $3/4$ cup chopped red sweet pepper (1 medium)
- $1/4$ cup snipped fresh cilantro

1. Rinse beans. Place beans in a large saucepan or Dutch oven. Add enough water to cover by 2 inches. Bring to boiling; reduce heat. Simmer, uncovered, for 10 minutes. Remove from heat. Cover; let stand for 1 hour.

2. Meanwhile, in a large skillet, cook half of the meat and the onion in hot oil over medium-high heat until meat is brown. Transfer to a $3^{1}/_{2}$- or 4-quart slow cooker. Repeat with remaining meat. Stir tomato sauce, undrained tomatoes, beef broth, chipotle peppers and adobo sauce, oregano, and cumin into mixture in cooker. Drain and rinse the beans; stir into mixture in cooker.

3. Cover and cook on low-heat setting for 10 to 12 hours or on high-heat setting for 5 to 6 hours. Top each serving with red sweet pepper and fresh cilantro. Makes 8 (1-cup) servings.

*Test Kitchen Tip: Because chile peppers contain volatile oils that can burn your skin and eyes, avoid direct contact with them as much as possible. When working with chile peppers, wear plastic or rubber gloves. If your bare hands do touch the peppers, wash your hands and nails well with soap and water.

Hearty Beef Chili

Please your guests with a chili bar. They'll have fun choosing toppings to taste.

PER SERVING: 206 cal., 4 g total fat (1 g sat. fat), 37 mg chol., 565 mg sodium, 24 g carb., 7 g fiber, 22 g pro. Exchanges: 2 vegetable, 1 starch, 2 very lean meat. Carb choices: 1.5.

- 2 14-ounce cans no-salt-added diced tomatoes, undrained
- 1 10-ounce can chopped tomatoes and green chile peppers, undrained
- 2 cups vegetable juice or tomato juice
- 1 to 2 tablespoons chili powder
- 1 teaspoon ground cumin
- 1 teaspoon dried oregano, crushed
- 3 cloves garlic, minced
- $1^{1}/_{2}$ pounds beef or pork stew meat, cut into 1-inch cubes
- 2 cups chopped onion
- $1^{1}/_{2}$ cups chopped celery
- 1 cup chopped green sweet pepper
- 2 15-ounce cans black beans, kidney beans, and/or garbanzo beans (chickpeas), rinsed and drained

  Toppings (such as shredded reduced-fat cheddar cheese, light dairy sour cream, snipped fresh cilantro, and/or pitted ripe olives) (optional)

1. In a 6-quart slow cooker, combine canned tomatoes, vegetable juice, chili powder, cumin, oregano, and garlic. Stir in meat, onion, celery, and sweet pepper.

2. Cover and cook on low-heat setting for 8 to 10 hours or on high-heat setting for 4 to 5 hours.

3. If using low-heat setting, turn to high-heat setting. Stir in the drained beans. Cover and cook for 15 minutes more. If desired, top each serving with desired toppings. Makes 10 ($1^{1}/_{2}$-cup) servings.

Hearty Beef Chili

Sloppy Joes with a Kick

A couple of sassy ingredients—hot-style tomato juice and jalapeño peppers—give these sandwiches a lively twist.

PER SANDWICH: 310 cal., 13 g total fat (5 g sat. fat), 53 mg chol., 522 mg sodium, 27 g carb., 3 g fiber, 21 g pro. Exchanges: 2 starch, 2 lean meat, 2 fat. Carb choices: 2.

- 1¹/₂ pounds lean ground beef
- 1 cup chopped onion
- 1 clove garlic, minced
- 1 6-ounce can vegetable juice
- ¹/₂ cup ketchup
- 2 tablespoons sugar substitute*
- 2 tablespoons chopped canned jalapeño peppers (see tip, at right) (optional)
- 1 tablespoon prepared mustard
- 2 teaspoons chili powder
- 1 teaspoon Worcestershire sauce
- 8 whole wheat hamburger buns, split and toasted
  Shredded reduced-fat cheddar cheese (optional)

1. In a large skillet, cook ground beef, onion, and garlic until meat is brown and onion is tender. Drain off fat.

2. Meanwhile, in a 3¹/₂- or 4-quart slow cooker, combine vegetable juice, ketchup, ¹/₂ cup *water,* sugar substitute, jalapeño peppers (if desired), mustard, chili powder, and Worcestershire sauce. Stir in meat mixture.

3. Cover and cook on low-heat setting for 6 to 8 hours or on high-heat setting for 3 to 4 hours. Spoon meat mixture onto bun halves. If desired, sprinkle with cheese. Makes 8 sandwiches.

*Sugar Substitutes: Choose from Splenda granular, Equal Spoonful or packets, or Sweet'N Low bulk or packets.

Sloppy Joes with a Kick

Beef and Chipotle Burritos

Canned chipotle peppers are smoked jalapeños that lend a smoky flavor to foods.

PER SERVING: 313 cal., 8 g total fat (2 g sat. fat), 49 mg chol., 704 mg sodium, 27 g carb., 3 g fiber, 31 g pro. Exchanges: 0.5 vegetable, 0.5 starch, 4 very lean meat, 1 fat. Carb choices: 2.

- 1¹/₂ pounds boneless beef round steak, cut ³/₄ inch thick
- 1 14¹/₂-ounce can low-sodium diced tomatoes
- ¹/₃ cup chopped red onion
- 1 to 2 canned chipotle chile peppers in adobo sauce, chopped*
- 1 teaspoon dried oregano, crushed
- 1 clove garlic, minced
- ¹/₄ teaspoon salt
- ¹/₄ teaspoon ground cumin
- 6 6- to 7-inch whole wheat or low-fat flour tortillas, warmed
- ³/₄ cup shredded reduced-fat cheddar cheese (3 ounces) (optional)
- 1 recipe Pico de Gallo Salsa (below) (optional)

1. Trim fat from meat. Cut meat into 6 pieces. In a 3¹/₂- or 4-quart slow cooker, place meat, undrained tomatoes, onion, chipotle peppers, oregano, garlic, salt, and cumin.

2. Cover and cook on low-heat setting for 8 to 10 hours or on high-heat setting for 4 to 5 hours.

3. Remove meat from slow cooker; reserve cooking liquid. Using two forks, pull meat apart into shreds. Stir enough reserved cooking liquid into meat to moisten.

4. To serve, spoon meat just below centers of tortillas. If desired, top with cheese and Pico de Gallo Salsa. Roll up tortillas. Makes 6 servings.

Pico de Gallo Salsa: In a small bowl, combine 1 cup finely chopped tomatoes, 2 tablespoons finely chopped red onion, 2 tablespoons snipped fresh cilantro, and 1 seeded and finely chopped fresh serrano pepper.* Stir in ¹/₂ cup chopped, peeled jicama and ¹/₄ cup thin strips radishes. Cover and chill salsa for several hours before serving.

*Test Kitchen Tip: Because chile peppers contain volatile oils that can burn your skin and eyes, avoid direct contact with them as much as possible. When working with chile peppers, wear plastic or rubber gloves. If your bare hands do touch the peppers, wash your hands and nails well with soap and warm water.

Quick Tip

To tote slow-cooker foods, wrap the cooker in heavy foil, several layers of newspapers, or a heavy towel. Place cooker in an insulated container. The food should stay hot for up to 2 hours (do not hold longer than 2 hours).

Beef and Chipotle Burritos

Spiced Pot Roast with Root Vegetables

Spiced Pot Roast with Root Vegetables

Garam masala is a blend of ground dry-roasted spices. The blend varies and can include pepper, cloves, cinnamon, cumin, chiles, fennel, and other spices. Buy garam masala where Indian foods are sold.

PER SERVING: 274 cal., 7 g total fat (2 g sat. fat), 82 mg chol., 381 mg sodium, 18 g carb., 3 g fiber, 32 g pro. Exchanges: 0.5 vegetable, 1 starch, 4 very lean meat, 1 fat. Carb choices: 1.

- 1   3-pound boneless beef chuck pot roast
- 3¹/₂ teaspoons garam masala
- ³/₄   teaspoon salt
- 1   tablespoon cooking oil
- 1   cup beef broth
- ¹/₄   cup dry red wine or beef broth
- 30 small carrots with tops (about 12 ounces) or 2 cups peeled baby carrots
- 1   pound round red potatoes, quartered
- 2   medium parsnips, peeled and cut into ¹/₂-inch-thick slices
- 1   medium rutabaga, peeled and cut into 1-inch pieces
- 1   red onion, cut into wedges
- 2   tablespoons cornstarch
- 2   tablespoons cold water
- ¹/₄   teaspoon ground black pepper
- 1   cup plain low-fat yogurt

1. Trim fat from roast. For rub, in a bowl, combine 2¹/₂ teaspoons of the garam masala and ¹/₂ teaspoon of the salt; rub onto meat.

2. In a 4-quart Dutch oven, cook meat in hot oil until brown, turning as needed. Drain off fat.

3. Place meat in a 5- to 6-quart slow cooker. Top with the 1 cup broth, the wine, carrots, potatoes, parsnips, rutabaga, and onion.

4. Cover and cook on low-heat setting for 10 to 12 hours or on high-heat setting for 5 to 6 hours. Transfer meat and vegetables to a serving platter.

5. For gravy, skim and discard fat from cooking liquid; strain liquid. Measure 1¹/₂ cups liquid (discard remaining liquid); place in Dutch oven.

6. In a small bowl, stir together cornstarch, cold water, remaining 1 teaspoon garam masala, remaining ¹/₂ teaspoon salt, and the pepper; add to Dutch oven. Cook and stir over medium heat until thickened and bubbly. Cook and stir for 2 minutes more. Stir in yogurt; heat through but do not boil. Serve gravy with meat and vegetables. Makes 10 servings.

Cajun Pot Roast with Sweet Peppers

If you're watching sodium intake, read the label on the Cajun seasoning to make sure it's salt-free.

PER SERVING: 174 cal., 5 g total fat (2 g sat. fat), 67 mg chol., 86 mg sodium, 6 g carb., 2 g fiber, 25 g pro. Exchanges: 1 vegetable, 3 very lean meat, 1 fat. Carb choices: 0.5.

- 1 2- to 2½-pound boneless beef chuck (pot) roast
- 1 tablespoon salt-free Cajun seasoning or Homemade Cajun Salt-Free Seasoning (see recipe, page 132)
- ½ teaspoon bottled hot pepper sauce
- ⅛ teaspoon ground black pepper
- 1 14.5-ounce can low-sodium diced tomatoes
- 1 medium green sweet pepper, cut into strips
- 1 medium red sweet pepper, cut into strips
- 1 medium yellow sweet pepper, cut into strips
- Cracked black pepper (optional)

1. Trim fat from meat. Sprinkle Cajun seasoning evenly onto meat; rub in with your fingers. If necessary, cut meat to fit into a 3½- or 4-quart slow cooker.

2. Place meat in slow cooker. Add pepper sauce and ⅛ teaspoon black pepper. Add undrained tomatoes.

3. Cover and cook on low-heat setting for 8 to 10 hours or on high-heat setting for 4 to 5 hours, adding pepper strips the last 30 minutes of cooking.

4. Transfer meat to a cutting board. Slice meat; transfer to a platter. Drain vegetables, discarding cooking liquid. Serve meat with vegetables. If desired, sprinkle with cracked pepper. Makes 8 servings.

Dilled Pot Roast

This company-worthy dish will remind you of stroganoff with its savory dilled yogurt sauce.

PER SERVING: 313 cal., 8 g total fat (2 g sat. fat), 111 mg chol., 185 mg sodium, 22 g carb., 1 g fiber, 35 g pro. Exchanges: 1.5 starch, 4.5 very lean meat, 1 fat. Carb choices: 1.5.

- 1 2½- to 3-pound boneless beef chuck pot roast
- 1 tablespoon cooking oil
- ½ cup water
- 1 tablespoon snipped fresh dill or 1 teaspoon dried dill
- ½ teaspoon ground black pepper
- ¼ teaspoon salt
- ½ cup plain low-fat yogurt
- 2 tablespoons all-purpose flour
- 4 cups hot cooked noodles

1. If necessary, cut roast to fit into a 3½- or 4-quart slow cooker. In a large skillet, brown roast on all sides in hot oil. Transfer roast to slow cooker; add the water. Sprinkle roast with 2 teaspoons of the fresh dill or ¾ teaspoon of the dried dill, pepper, and salt.

2. Cover and cook on low-heat setting for 10 to 12 hours or on high-heat setting for 5 to 6 hours.

3. Transfer roast to a platter, reserving juices; cover and keep warm. Pour juices into a glass measuring cup; skim off fat. Measure 1 cup reserved juices.

4. For sauce, in a small saucepan, stir together yogurt and flour. Stir in the 1 cup reserved cooking juices and remaining 1 teaspoon fresh dill or ¼ teaspoon dried dill. Cook and stir over medium-low heat until thickened and bubbly. Cook and stir for 1 minute more. Serve sauce with meat and noodles. Makes 8 servings.

So-Easy Pepper Steak

Choose the stewed-tomato flavoring that fits your party's theme or your guests' preferences.

PER SERVING: 196 cal., 5 g total fat (2 g sat. fat), 54 mg chol., 411 mg sodium, 9 g carb., 1 g fiber, 27 g pro. Exchanges: 1.5 vegetable, 3.5 very lean meat, 1 fat. Carb choices: 0.5.

- 2 pounds boneless beef round steak, cut ¾ to 1 inch thick
- ⅛ teaspoon salt
- ⅛ teaspoon ground black pepper
- 1 14.5-ounce can Cajun-, Mexican-, or Italian-style stewed tomatoes
- ⅓ cup tomato paste with Italian seasoning
- ½ teaspoon bottled hot pepper sauce
- 1 16-ounce package frozen pepper stir-fry vegetables (yellow, green, and red peppers with onion)
- 4 cups hot cooked whole wheat pasta (optional)

1. Trim fat from meat. Cut meat into serving-size pieces. Sprinkle with salt and black pepper. Place meat in a 3½- or 4-quart slow cooker.

2. In a medium bowl, combine undrained tomatoes, tomato paste, and hot pepper sauce. Pour tomato mixture over meat in cooker. Top with frozen vegetables.

3. Cover and cook on low-heat setting for 10 to 12 hours or on high-heat setting for 5 to 6 hours. Serve with hot cooked pasta. Makes 8 servings.

Pasta with Eggplant-Tomato Sauce

Tender chunks of eggplant replace ground beef or sausage in this pasta sauce.

PER SERVING: 231 cal., 2g total fat (1 g sat. fat), 3 mg chol., 584 mg sodium, 44 g carb., 5 g fiber, 9 g pro. Exchanges: 2 starch, 3 vegetable. Carb choices: 3.

- 1 medium eggplant
- 1/2 cup chopped onion (1 medium)
- 1 28-ounce can Italian-style tomatoes, undrained and cut up
- 1 6-ounce can Italian-style tomato paste
- 1 4-ounce can sliced mushrooms, drained
- 2 cloves garlic, minced
- 1/4 cup dry red wine
- 1/4 cup water
- 1 1/2 teaspoons dried oregano, crushed
- 1/3 cup pitted ripe olives, sliced (optional)
- 2 tablespoons snipped fresh parsley
- 4 cups hot cooked penne pasta
- 1/4 cup grated or shredded Parmesan cheese

Pasta with Eggplant-Tomato Sauce

1. Peel eggplant, if desired; cut eggplant into 1-inch cubes. In a 3 1/2- to 5 1/2-quart slow cooker, combine eggplant, onion, undrained tomatoes, tomato paste, drained mushrooms, garlic, wine, water, and oregano.

2. Cover and cook on low-heat setting for 7 to 8 hours or on high-heat setting for 3 1/2 to 4 hours. Stir in olives and parsley. Serve over pasta; sprinkle with Parmesan cheese. Makes 6 servings.

Meatless Burritos

Everyone likes burritos, and this recipe makes enough to serve a crowd. For easy serve-alongs, pick up a fruit salad from the deli and a package or two of Mexican-style rice mix.

PER SERVING: 205 cal., 3 g total fat (2 g sat. fat), 7 mg chol., 471 mg sodium, 34 g carb., 6 g fiber, 8 g pro. Exchanges: 0.5 vegetable, 2 starch, 0.5 very lean meat. Carb choices: 2.

- 3 15-ounce cans red kidney and/or black beans, rinsed and drained
- 1 14.5-ounce can diced tomatoes, undrained
- 1 1/2 cups bottled salsa or picante sauce
- 1 11-ounce can whole kernel corn with sweet peppers, drained
- 1 fresh jalapeño chile pepper, seeded and finely chopped (optional) (see tip, page 146)
- 2 teaspoons chili powder
- 2 cloves garlic, minced
- 16 8- to 10-inch flour tortillas, warmed
- 2 cups shredded lettuce
- 1 cup shredded taco cheese or cheddar cheese (4 ounces)
  Sliced green onions and/or dairy sour cream (optional)

1. In a 3 1/2- or 4-quart slow cooker combine beans, undrained tomatoes, salsa, corn, jalapeño pepper (if desired), chili powder, and garlic.

2. Cover and cook on low-heat setting for 6 to 8 hours or on high-heat setting for 3 to 4 hours.

3. To serve, spoon bean mixture just below centers of tortillas. Top with lettuce and cheese. If desired, top with green onions and/or sour cream. Fold bottom edge of each tortilla up and over filling. Fold in opposite sides; roll up from bottom. Makes 16 (1-cup bean mixture and 1-tortilla) servings.

Vegetable Stew with Cornmeal Dumplings

Watch the dumplings through the transparent cooker lid as they cook. Resist lifting the lid; if you do, the biscuits will take longer to cook.

PER SERVING: 288 cal., 7 g total fat (2 g sat. fat), 37 mg chol., 442 mg sodium, 45 g carb., 7 g fiber, 12 g prot. Exchanges: 2.5 starch, 2 vegetable, 1 fat. Carb choices: 3.

- 3 cups peeled butternut or acorn squash cut into 1/2-inch cubes
- 2 cups sliced fresh mushrooms
- 2 14.5-ounce cans diced tomatoes
- 1 15-ounce can Great Northern beans, drained
- 1 cup water
- 4 cloves garlic, minced
- 1 teaspoon dried Italian seasoning, crushed
- 1/4 teaspoon ground black pepper
- 1/2 cup all-purpose flour
- 1/3 cup cornmeal
- 2 tablespoons grated Parmesan cheese
- 1 tablespoon snipped fresh parsley
- 1 teaspoon baking powder
- 1/4 teaspoon salt
- 1 beaten egg
- 2 tablespoons milk
- 2 tablespoons cooking oil
- 1 9-ounce package frozen Italian green beans or frozen cut green beans
  Paprika

1. In a 3 1/2- or 4-quart slow cooker, combine squash, mushrooms, undrained tomatoes, Great Northern beans, water, garlic, Italian seasoning, and pepper.

2. Cover and cook on low-heat setting for 8 to 10 hours or on high-heat setting for 4 to 5 hours.

3. Meanwhile, for dumplings, in a medium bowl, stir together flour, cornmeal, Parmesan cheese, parsley, baking powder, and salt. In a small bowl, combine egg, milk, and oil. Add to the flour mixture; stir with a fork just until combined.

4. If using low-heat setting, turn to high-heat setting. Stir frozen Italian green beans into stew. Drop dumpling mixture by tablespoons on top of stew. Sprinkle dumplings with paprika. Cover and cook for 50 minutes more on high-heat setting, leaving the cover on during the entire cooking time. Makes 6 (1 1/4-cup stew and 2-dumpling) servings.

Mushroom Goulash

Goulash is typically a meaty dish flavored with paprika and served with noodles. This version does not include meat.

PER SERVING: 251 cal., 5 g total fat (2 g sat. fat), 43 mg chol., 443 mg sodium, 43 g carb., 5 g fiber, 12 g pro. Exchanges: 2 starch, 2 vegetable 1 fat. Carb choices: 3.

- 16 ounces fresh baby portobello mushrooms, sliced
- 1 tablespoon dried minced onion
- 3 cloves garlic, minced
- 1 14-ounce can vegetable broth
- 1 14.5-ounce can no-salt-added diced tomatoes, undrained
- 1 6-ounce can no-salt added tomato paste
- 2 tablespoons paprika
- 1 teaspoon dried oregano, crushed
- 1 teaspoon caraway seeds
- 1/4 teaspoon salt
- 1/4 teaspoon ground black pepper
- 1/2 cup light dairy sour cream
- 8 ounces dried egg noodles, cooked and drained

1. In a 3 1/2- to 4-quart slow cooker, combine mushrooms, onion, and garlic. Stir in broth, undrained tomatoes, tomato paste, paprika, oregano, caraway seeds, salt, and pepper.

2. Cover and cook on low-heat setting for 8 to 9 hours or on high-heat setting for 4 to 4 1/2 hours.

3. Stir sour cream into mushroom mixture before serving. Serve with hot noodles. Makes 6 (scant 1-cup) servings.

managing your diabetes

Understanding diabetes gives you a better chance of controlling it and preventing complications. It pays to learn all you can, then develop a plan that fits your lifestyle.

An estimated 21 million people in the United States, or 7 percent of the U.S. population, have diabetes, according to the Centers for Disease Control and Prevention. An additional 54 million Americans have pre-diabetes—indicating an increased risk of developing diabetes. If you're one of them, remember that you—not your doctor, dietitian, or other health professional—play the most important role in staying healthy.

Define Your Diabetes
Your health-care team will work with you to develop a personalized diabetes management plan, consisting of healthful foods, physical activity, and, if necessary, the medication that's right for you and your type of diabetes (type 1, type 2, or gestational).

Type 1 diabetes: In this type, the pancreas doesn't produce insulin, so people with type 1 diabetes must take insulin. A typical treatment plan begins with an individualized meal plan, guidelines for physical activity, and blood glucose testing. Insulin therapy is then planned around lifestyle and eating patterns.

Type 2 diabetes: In type 2 diabetes, either the pancreas doesn't produce enough insulin or the body doesn't properly respond to insulin, so too much glucose remains in the blood. Many people control type 2 diabetes by following a specially designed meal plan and engaging in regular physical activity. The right plan can help people reach and attain a desirable weight, plus healthy blood glucose, blood cholesterol, and blood pressure levels. As the disease progresses, treatment may expand to include oral medications, oral medications with insulin, or insulin alone.

Gestational diabetes: This type develops only during pregnancy. Women who've had gestational diabetes have a higher risk of developing type 2 diabetes.

Develop Your Meal Plan
Adhering to a healthful meal plan is one of the most important measures you can take to control your blood glucose. Work with a dietitian to design a meal plan that reflects your individual needs and preferences. Your meal plan should also:

* Include fruits, vegetables, and whole grains.
* Reduce the amount of saturated fat and cholesterol you eat.
* Minimize the amount of salt or sodium you eat.
* Incorporate a moderate amount of sugar because some sugar can be part of a healthful diabetes meal plan.
* Help you maintain or achieve an ideal weight.

Follow Your Meal Plan
As you start following your meal plan, you'll see that it gives you some flexibility regarding what, how much, and when you eat, but you have to be comfortable with the foods it suggests. It will guide you in eating appropriate amounts of three major nutrients—carbohydrates, protein, and fat—at the right times. Your meal plan will be nutritionally balanced, allowing you to get the vitamins, minerals, and fiber your body needs. And if you need to lose weight, it will indicate how many calories you should consume every day in order to lose the extra pounds at a realistic pace.

Your meal plan can be simple, especially if you use a proven technique to keep track of what you're eating. Two well-known meal-planning systems for diabetes are diabetic exchanges and carbohydrate counting. Your dietitian may suggest one or the other. To help you follow either system, every recipe in this book provides nutrition information, including the number of exchanges and carb choices in each serving. (Turn to page 155 to see how to use this information.)

Track the Exchanges

Exchange Lists for Meal Planning outlines a system designed by the American Diabetes Association and the American Dietetic Association. To use the exchange system, your dietitian will work with you to develop a pattern of food exchanges—or a meal plan—suited to your specific needs. You'll be able to keep track of the number of exchanges from various food groups that you eat each day. Tally those numbers and match the total

to the daily allowance set in your meal plan. (For more information, visit *diabetes.org*.)

Count Carbohydrates

Carbohydrate counting is the method many diabetes educators prefer for keeping tabs on what you eat. It makes sense because the carbohydrate content of foods has the greatest effect on

blood glucose levels. If you focus on carbohydrates, you can eat a variety of foods and still control your blood glucose.

When counting carbohydrates, you can tally the number of grams you eat each day. Or you can count the number of carbohydrate choices, which allows you to work with smaller numbers. We offer both numbers with our recipes.

Basic carbohydrate counting relies on eating about the same amount of carbohydrates at the same times each day to keep blood glucose levels in your target range. It's a good meal-planning method if you have type 2 diabetes and take no daily oral diabetes medications or take one to two shots of insulin per day.

Advanced carbohydrate counting is a more complex method than the basic system of carbohydrate counting. It's designed for individuals who take multiple daily insulin injections or use an insulin pump. With advanced carbohydrate counting, you have to balance the amount of carbohydrates you consume with the insulin you take. You estimate the amount of carbohydrates you'll be eating and adjust your mealtime insulin dose based on your recommended insulin-to-carbohydrate ratio. To learn how to follow advanced carbohydrate counting, seek the assistance of a registered dietitian or certified diabetes educator.

The Carbohydrate Question

Although the calories from fat, protein, and carbohydrates all affect your blood glucose level, carbohydrates affect it the most. So why not just avoid carbohydrates altogether? While carbohydrates may be the main nutrient that raises blood glucose levels, you shouldn't cut them from your diet. Foods that contain carbohydrates are among the most healthful available—vegetables, fruits, whole grains, and low-fat or nonfat dairy foods. Eliminating these foods could compromise your health.

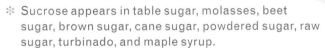

(be a sugar sleuth)

Knowing the different forms of sugar can make life sweeter when you're reading labels and recipes. Sugar content is included in the total grams we list for carbohydrates in recipes.

❉ Sucrose appears in table sugar, molasses, beet sugar, brown sugar, cane sugar, powdered sugar, raw sugar, turbinado, and maple syrup.
❉ Other "-ose" sugars include glucose (or dextrose), fructose, lactose, and maltose. Fructose and sugar alcohols affect blood glucose less than sucrose, but large amounts of fructose may increase blood fat levels.
❉ Sugar alcohols such as sorbitol, xylitol, maltitol, mannitol, lactitol, and erythritol should only be eaten in moderation because they can cause diarrhea, gas, and cramping.

How Sweet It Is

For many years, people with diabetes were told to shun sugar because it was thought that sugar caused blood glucose to soar out of control. So they diligently wiped sugary foods and sugar out of their diets, hoping to stabilize their blood glucose levels. Today, more than a dozen studies have shown sugars in foods don't cause blood glucose to spike any higher or faster than starches, such as those in potatoes and bread. The American Diabetes Association's recommendations on sugar now state "scientific evidence has shown that the use of sucrose (table sugar) as part of the meal plan does not impair blood glucose control in individuals with type 1 or type 2 diabetes."

It is important to note, however, that sugar is not a "free food." It still contains calories and offers no nutritional value beyond providing energy. When you eat foods that contain sugar, they have to replace other carbohydrate-rich foods in your meal plan. Carbohydrates you eat contain a healthful amount of vitamins, minerals, and fiber. So it's a good idea to focus on whole grains and vegetables for your carbohydrates rather than sugar. Talk to your dietitian to determine a healthful way to include a moderate amount of sugar in your meal plan. Or you can also sweeten foods with sugar substitutes (see "Low-Calorie Sweeteners," page 153).

Stay Involved and Informed

Eating healthfully, exercising, and monitoring blood glucose levels help keep diabetes in check—all easier to do if you follow the plans you've developed with your health-care providers. Update them on your progress and request changes if something isn't working. And stay informed about diabetes by going to *diabeticlivingonline.com* to sign up for our e-mail newsletter. You're the one who can monitor your progress day by day.

(using our nutrition information)

At the top of every one of our recipes, you'll see the nutrition information listed for each serving. You'll find the amount of calories (cal.), total fat, saturated fat (sat. fat), cholesterol (chol.), sodium, total carbohydrates (carb.), fiber, and protein (pro.). In addition, you'll find the number of diabetic exchanges for each serving and the number of carbohydrate choices, in case you prefer those methods to keep track of what you're eating.

PER SERVING: 134 cal., 9 g total fat (1 g sat. fat), 0 mg chol., 60 mg sodium, 14 g carb., 4 g fiber, 2 g pro. Exchanges: 0.5 fruit, 1 vegetable, 2 fat. Carb choices: 1.

Interpreting the Numbers
Use our nutrition analyses to keep track of the nutritional value of the foods you eat, following the meal plan you and your dietitian have decided is right for you. Refer to that plan to see how a recipe fits the number of diabetic exchanges or carbohydrate choices you're allotted for each day. When

you try a recipe, jot down our nutrition numbers to keep a running tally of what you're eating, remembering your daily allowances. At the end of each day, see how your numbers compare to your plan.

Diabetic Exchanges
The exchange system allows you to choose from a variety of items within several food groupings. Those groupings include starch, fruit, fat-free milk, carbohydrates, nonstarchy vegetables, meat and meat substitutes, fat, and free foods. To use the diabetic exchange system with our recipes, follow your plan's recommendations on the number of servings you should select from each exchange group in a day.

Carbohydrate Counting
Our recipes help you keep track of carbohydrates in two ways—tallying grams of carbohydrates and the number of carbohydrate choices. For counting grams, add the amounts of total carbohydrates to your running total for the day. For carbohydrate choices,

one choice equals 15 grams of carbohydrates. For example, a sandwich made with two slices of bread is 2 carbohydrate choices. The benefit of this system is that you're keeping track of small numbers.

Calculating Method
To calculate our nutrition information and offer flexibility in our recipes, we've made some decisions about what's included in our analyses and what's not. We follow these guidelines when we analyze recipes that list ingredient options or serving suggestions:

* When ingredient choices appear (such as yogurt or sour cream), we use the first one mentioned for the analysis.
* When an ingredient is listed as optional, such as a garnish or a suggested serve-along, we don't include it in our nutrition analysis.
* When we offer a range in the number of servings, we use the smaller number.
* For marinades, we assume most of it is discarded.

recipe index

metric information

The charts on this page provide a guide for converting measurements from the U.S. customary system, which is used throughout this book, to the metric system.

Product Differences

Most of the ingredients called for in the recipes in this book are available in most countries. However, some are known by different names. Here are some common American ingredients and their possible counterparts:

❃ All-purpose flour is enriched, bleached or unbleached white household flour. When self-rising flour is used in place of all-purpose flour in a recipe that calls for leavening, omit the leavening agent (baking soda or baking powder) and salt.
❃ Baking soda is bicarbonate of soda.
❃ Cornstarch is cornflour.
❃ Golden raisins are sultanas.
❃ Light-colored corn syrup is golden syrup.
❃ Powdered sugar is icing sugar.
❃ Sugar (white) is granulated, fine granulated, or castor sugar.
❃ Vanilla or vanilla extract is vanilla essence.

Volume and Weight

The United States traditionally uses cup measures for liquid and solid ingredients. The chart below shows the approximate imperial and metric equivalents. If you are accustomed to weighing solid ingredients, the following approximate equivalents will be helpful.

❃ 1 cup butter, castor sugar, or rice = 8 ounces = ½ pound = 250 grams
❃ 1 cup flour = 4 ounces = ¼ pound = 125 grams
❃ 1 cup icing sugar = 5 ounces = 150 grams

Canadian and U.S. volume for a cup measure is 8 fluid ounces (237 ml), but the standard metric equivalent is 250 ml.

1 British imperial cup is 10 fluid ounces.

In Australia, 1 tablespoon equals 20 ml, and there are 4 teaspoons in the Australian tablespoon.

Spoon measures are used for smaller amounts of ingredients. Although the size of the tablespoon varies slightly in different countries, for practical purposes and for recipes in this book, a straight substitution is all that's necessary. Measurements made using cups or spoons always should be level unless stated otherwise.

Common Weight Range Replacements

Imperial / U.S.	Metric
½ ounce	15 g
1 ounce	25 g or 30 g
4 ounces (¼ pound)	115 g or 125 g
8 ounces (½ pound)	225 g or 250 g
16 ounces (1 pound)	450 g or 500 g
1¼ pounds	625 g
1½ pounds	750 g
2 pounds or 2¼ pounds	1,000 g or 1 Kg

Oven Temperature Equivalents

Fahrenheit Setting	Celsius Setting*	Gas Setting
300°F	150°C	Gas Mark 2 (very low)
325°F	160°C	Gas Mark 3 (low)
350°F	180°C	Gas Mark 4 (moderate)
375°F	190°C	Gas Mark 5 (moderate)
400°F	200°C	Gas Mark 6 (hot)
425°F	220°C	Gas Mark 7 (hot)
450°F	230°C	Gas Mark 8 (very hot)
475°F	240°C	Gas Mark 9 (very hot)
500°F	260°C	Gas Mark 10 (extremely hot)
Broil	Broil	Grill

*Electric and gas ovens may be calibrated using celsius. However, for an electric oven, increase celsius setting 10 to 20 degrees when cooking above 160°C. For convection or forced air ovens (gas or electric), lower the temperature setting 25°F/10°C when cooking at all heat levels.

Baking Pan Sizes

Imperial / U.S.	Metric
9×1½-inch round cake pan	22- or 23×4-cm (1.5 L)
9×1½-inch pie plate	22- or 23×4-cm (1 L)
8×8×2-inch square cake pan	20×5-cm (2 L)
9×9×2-inch square cake pan	22- or 23×4.5-cm (2.5 L)
11×7×1½-inch baking pan	28×17×4-cm (2 L)
2-quart rectangular baking pan	30×19×4.5-cm (3 L)
13×9×2-inch baking pan	34×22×4.5-cm (3.5 L)
15×10×1-inch jelly roll pan	40×25×2-cm
9×5×3-inch loaf pan	23×13×8-cm (2 L)
2-quart casserole	2 L

U.S. / Standard Metric Equivalents

⅛ teaspoon = 0.5 ml	
¼ teaspoon = 1 ml	
½ teaspoon = 2 ml	
1 teaspoon = 5 ml	
1 tablespoon = 15 ml	
2 tablespoons = 25 ml	
¼ cup = 2 fluid ounces = 50 ml	
⅓ cup = 3 fluid ounces = 75 ml	
½ cup = 4 fluid ounces = 125 ml	
⅔ cup = 5 fluid ounces = 150 ml	
¾ cup = 6 fluid ounces = 175 ml	
1 cup = 8 fluid ounces = 250 ml	
2 cups = 1 pint = 500 ml	
1 quart = 1 litre	

DIABETIC LIVING™ series Holiday Cooking (ISBN 978-0-696-24254-0, ISSN 1943-2887), Volume 2. The DIABETIC LIVING cookbook series is published biannually by Meredith Corp., 1716 Locust St., Des Moines, IA 50309-3023. DIABETIC LIVING® magazine SUBSCRIPTION PRICES: U.S. and its possessions, 1 year $19.97; Canada and other countries, 1 year $23.97.